Devotions for Boys and Girls Ages 6 to 10

GOD'S AMAZING CREATURES

written by
Helen Haidle
illustrations by
Paul Haidle

First printing: August 2000
Fourth printing: June 2011

Master Books®, P.O. Box 726, Green Forest, AR 72638.

Master Books® is a division of the New Leaf Publishing Group, Inc.

ISBN 13: 978-0-89051-294-4
Library of Congress Catalog Card Number: 00-102738

All Scripture is from the New King James Version except where indicated. The New International Reader's Version has also been used to provide simplicity for the young readers.

Editorial consultant — Joshua Ramey

Cover by Farewell Communications

Printed in the United States of America

Please visit our website for other great titles:
www.masterbooks.net

For information regarding publicity
for author interviews
contact the publicity department at (870) 438-5288.

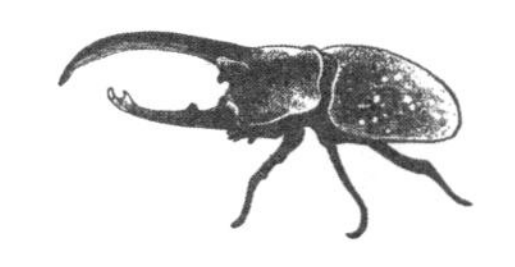

Dedication

To Peggy Kucera's students: Becky Dugan, Nick Dugan, Lisa Ellett, John Ellingson, Amanda Farmer, Nicole Jones, Victoria Jones, Matt Russell, Ashley Smith, and Alycia Harwood.

Thanks for all your enthusiastic reports on animals, birds, and fish!

To Jeannie Taylor, Alison Tenneson, and John Shepherd for critiques!

Special thanks to Rebekah Jordan for her writing and reports on "The Perfect Home" (page 16) and "Rejoice Always" (page 74).

To: Madelyne, Samuel, and Caroline
Merry Christmas 12-26-2012
May God Always Bless You
Love
Nanny & Papaw

Table of Contents

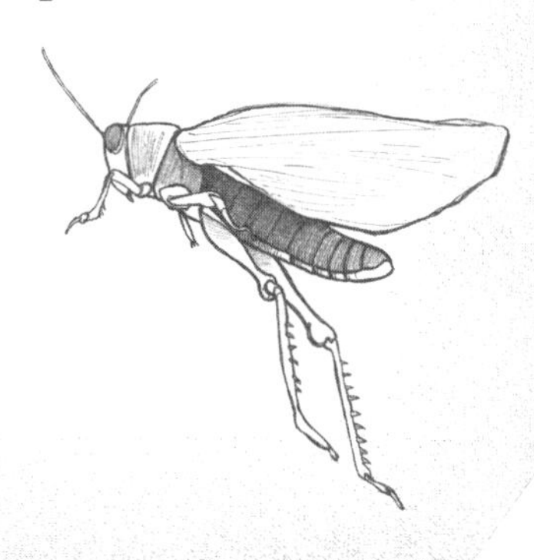

Jan 1, 2013

Follow a Good Example

For its size of body, the octopus has the largest brain of all animals without backbones. It is very intelligent and learns quickly. If trainers work with one octopus and teach it to do something, other octopuses will learn simply by watching. Some captive octopuses have even figured out how to escape from their tanks!

The octopus also has the best eyesight of all animals without backbones. When it searches for food, an octopus is a good judge of distance. If several crabs swim nearby, the octopus always makes the best choice and grabs the nearest crab with its muscular "arms," or tentacles.

An octopus, which is actually very shy, moves around the rocks and in the sand by crawling with its eight arms. The suction disks on their "arms" hang onto rocks.

The octopus can also swim with jet propulsion by forcing water out of a special funnel called a siphon. (That is like blowing up a balloon and letting it loose under water!)

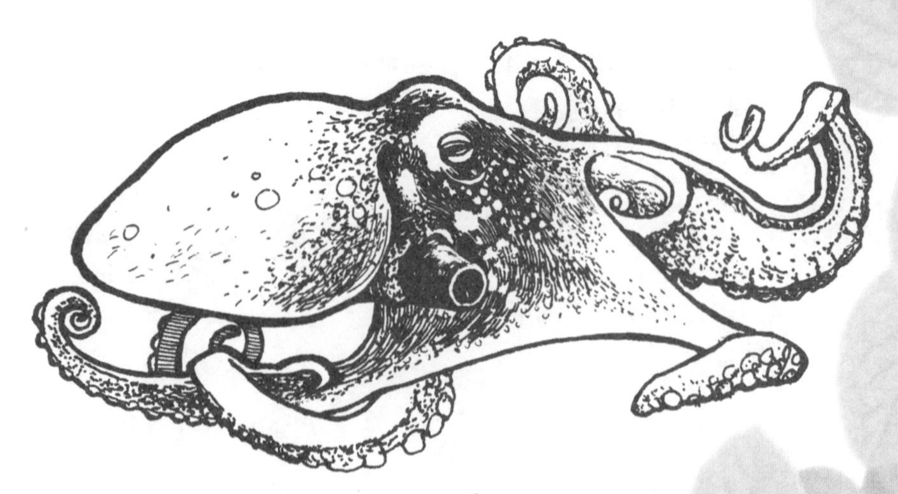

In the Bible . . .

Jesus' disciples learned by following Him. When Jesus first began his ministry, He told 12 men, "Come, follow me." And they did. They listened to Jesus teach. They watched Him heal many sick people. Then Jesus sent them out to do the same work of teaching and healing that He had done.

The night before Jesus was crucified, He washed His disciples' feet. He said, "I, your Lord and Teacher, have washed your feet. So you also should wash one another's feet. I have given you an example. You should do as I have done for you" (John 13:14–15;NIrV).

How about you?

How do you, like an octopus, learn by following? In what ways do you follow the good examples of your parents or teachers?

Are you willing to follow Jesus? Remember how Jesus treated other people? He took time for them. He helped them with their problems. He loved them. Think of one way you will follow Jesus' example today.

Memory Verse:

Jesus said, "For I have given you an example, that you should do as I have done to you."
(John 13:15)

Deadly Beauty

This is a beautiful fish with its shades of gold and reddish-brown colors. It is called by many names: the lionfish, devilfish, firefish, or zebrafish.

Although this lionfish looks almost angelic, its outward beauty is deceptive. The red and dark brown stripes on its lacy fins are one of nature's warnings. This pattern of stripes is a signal to other animals that they should beware!

Can you believe that this lovely fish is actually one of the most poisonous creatures in the sea? Each of the 18 spines that stick out of its body contains a poison gland in its long groove. The spines can cause painful wounds, which disable any fish that attack it. The lionfish's poison can also be fatal to humans.

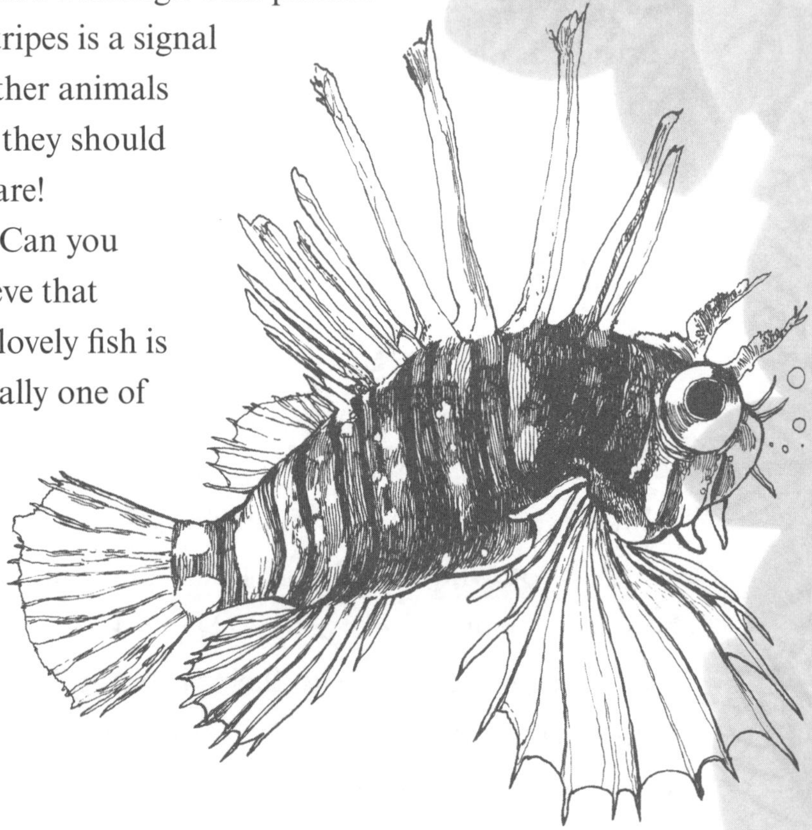

In the Bible . . .

Read the story of Adam and Eve in Genesis 2 and 3. God gave Adam and Eve everything they needed in the Garden of Eden. But God warned them, "You can eat the fruit of any tree that is in the garden. But you must not eat the fruit of the tree of the knowledge of good and evil. If you do, you can be sure that you will die" (Genesis 2:16-17;NIrV).

Why did Eve want to eat the fruit of "deadly beauty?" Why did she believe the serpent instead of God? What difference did her deadly choice make?

How about you?

Have you ever thought that something "looked" good, but you knew God didn't want you to do it? When has the devil tempted you to disobey God's laws? Don't fall into his deadly trap! Don't be deceived. Don't believe that you will enjoy something you shoplift or steal. More money will *not* make you happy. You don't have to smoke, do drugs, or join a gang in order to find friends.

Whenever you disobey God's laws, you are falling into the devil's trap of lies that lead to death.

Memory Verse:

Be sober, be vigilant; because your adversary the devil walks about like a roaring lion, seeking whom he may devour. Resist him, steadfast in the faith.
(1 Peter 5:8–9)

No Two Stripes Alike

A herd of zebras can play tricks on your eyes. Their stripes make it hard to tell where one animal begins and the other ends! These stripes also help confuse attackers who chase the herd.

Zebra roam in herds across the plains of Africa. It might seem like these horse-like creatures all look the same. The truth is — no two zebra's stripes are exactly alike!

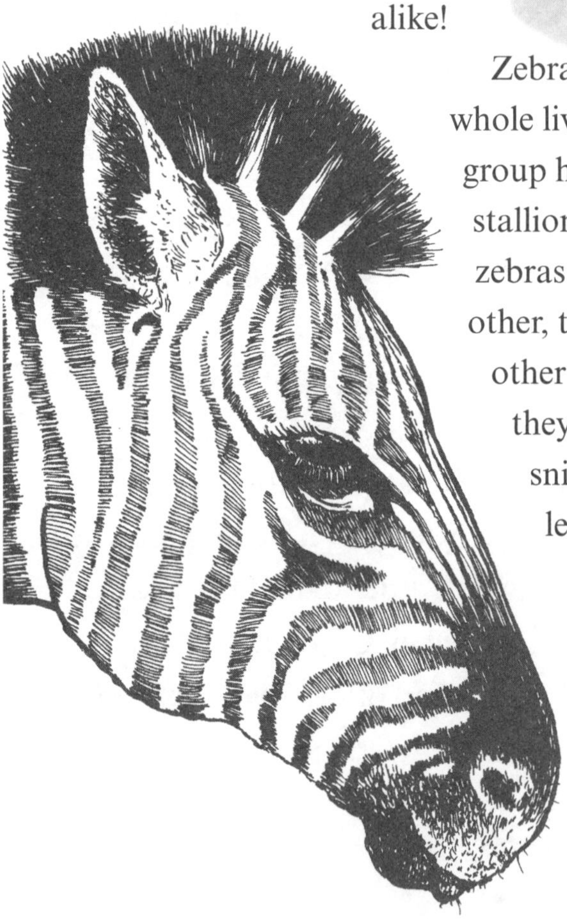

Zebras spend their whole lives in a family group headed by a stallion zebra. When zebras greet each other, they sniff each other's bellies. Then they rub chests, sniff noses, and leap away.

If a family group gets separated during an attack by a lion or another predator, they easily find each other again.

Adult zebras bray to those far away. When they are close enough again, zebras recognize each other by smell and also by sight. The young zebras always recognize their mother's stripes and know her smell.

In the Bible . . .

Just like each zebra has its own set of stripes, you are unique in God's eyes. God made each person to be a unique individual. God knew you in your mother's womb before you were even born. You are so important to God that He knew everything about you before anyone else had even seen you.

"For You formed my inward parts; You covered me in my mother's womb. I will praise You, for I am fearfully and wonderfully made; marvelous are Your works, and that my soul knows very well. My frame was not hidden from You, when I was made in secret" (Psalms 139:13–15).

Thank God that every person is different, yet equally important!

How about you?

Did you know that God has a unique plan for your life? God wants to use you to bless other people. What are some of the good things that *you* can do? Think of something special that you could do for your family today.

Ask yourself: How am I different from my friends or my brothers and sisters? How can God use *me* to bless others today?

Memory Verse:

O Lord, You have searched me and known me. You . . . are acquainted with all my ways (Psalm 139:1–3).

Don't Be a Quitter!

Emperor Penguins show us great examples of patient endurance. They live in the coldest place in the world — the Antarctic. They don't have any twigs or grass to build a nest, only miles and miles of ice and snow.

Penguins mate for life. The mother always lays her egg at the beginning of winter. Then she heads off to feed in the ocean.

The father penguin is a great dad. He holds his egg-baby on top of his toes. He keeps it off the ice so it won't freeze. A thick fold of skin on his belly hangs down like a blanket to cover the egg. All the egg-sitting fathers huddle together against winds as high as 100 miles per hour and temperatures as low as -70 degrees Fahrenheit. The father's body heat and warm flap of skin act like an insulated blanket for the egg.

This patient daddy holds his egg — day after day, week after week — for two months (60 days)! All this time he eats nothing. His body fat keeps him alive. He loses about one-third of his body weight!

When the baby pecks open its shell, the mother penguin returns. She will feed her newborn baby with fish that she regurgitates. Now the father heads to the ocean. He is hungry! After he eats his fill, he will bring back more fish for their baby.

What if this father quit caring for his egg on the 59th day because nothing *seemed to be* happening? The egg would freeze on the ice because its daddy gave up too soon.

In the Bible . . .

Elijah the prophet also teaches us not to quit! One, two, three, four, five, six times Elijah prayed for rain. He would not quit praying, not even when his servant kept telling him that there were no clouds in the sky.

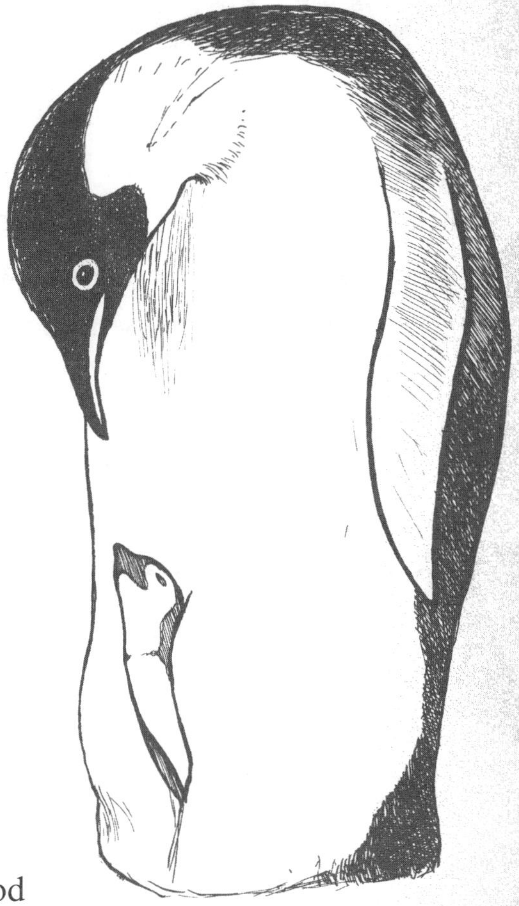

Finally, after Elijah's *seventh* prayer, his servant saw one small cloud in the distance. When Elijah heard that news, he jumped up and ran down the mountain. He knew that God would be answering his prayers for rain. And did it ever rain! (1 Kings 18:42–46).

How about you?

The more you love God and know God, the more you will talk to Him. If you are God's child, you can be sure God will keep His promise to answer your prayers . . . in God's own time. And it will be at the right time.

Don't give up or feel impatient when you don't receive an answer right away when you pray. Have you ever felt upset or stopped praying because it *seemed like* nothing was happening? Trust God. Wait patiently. And keep on praying.

Memory Verse:

Keep on praying.
(1 Thessalonians 5:17;NLT)

The Contented Cockroach

Have you ever seen a cockroach scurry across your kitchen floor? If they have ever invaded your house then you know they are hard to get rid of! They hide in warm, dark cracks and are very hard to catch. In these hidden places, one pair

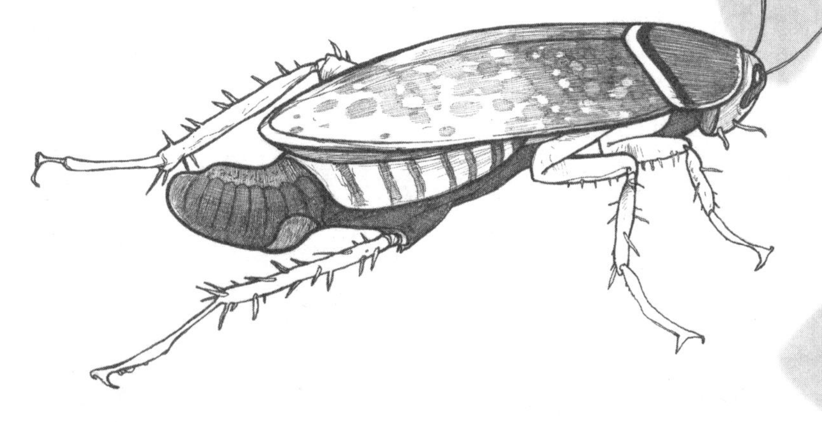

of cockroaches can lay 400,000 eggs each year.

Cockroaches feed mainly on vegetables and other foods, but the cockroach is content to eat almost anything it finds. They eat soap, paint, shoe polish, human garbage, and other dead cockroaches. They gobble up toenail and fingernail clippings!

Since cockroaches often search for food in dirty places, humans usually like to keep them out of their kitchens. Cockroaches are great survivors. They can even live three months without any food!

In the Bible . . .

God cares about people who are hungry. Once, God fed the prophet Elijah during a time of famine.

The king was searching for Elijah. He wanted to kill Elijah. So God told Elijah, "Hide by the Brook Cherith . . . you shall drink from the brook, and I have commanded the ravens to feed you there" (1 Kings 17:1–16).

Every morning and every night God sent birds to bring bread and meat to Elijah. Do you think Elijah ever complained about the food he got? Do you think he got tired of what God gave him? Or do you think he was content?

How about you?

Are you content with what you have? Do you complain about what you *don't* have? When you feel like complaining, it might help to think of the cockroach. They make do with whatever they find.

God never promised to give you everything you want. But we can still be content because God will make sure His children have what they need.

"My God will supply all your needs. He will meet them in keeping with his wonderful riches that come to you because you belong to Christ Jesus" (Philippians 4:19; NIrV).

Memory Verse:

Be content with such things as you have.
(Hebrews 13:5)

THE PERFECT HOME

When animal mothers get pregnant, they begin making a special home. They know exactly what their baby needs. They want a warm and protected place for their baby to be born.

This reed warbler makes a perfect home. It builds its nest high above swampy marsh water. It weaves grass, reed flowers, and feathers around tall dry reeds.

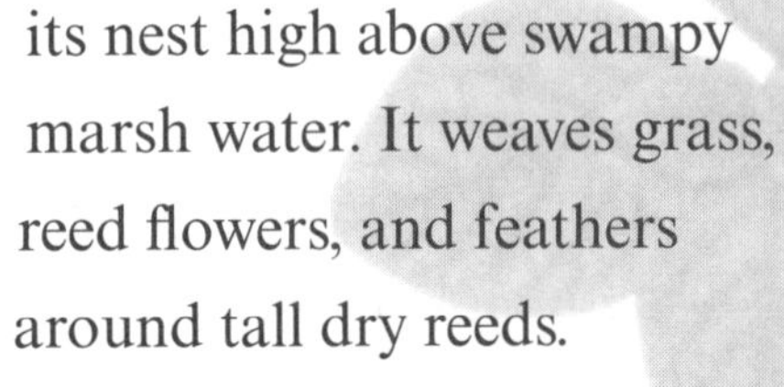

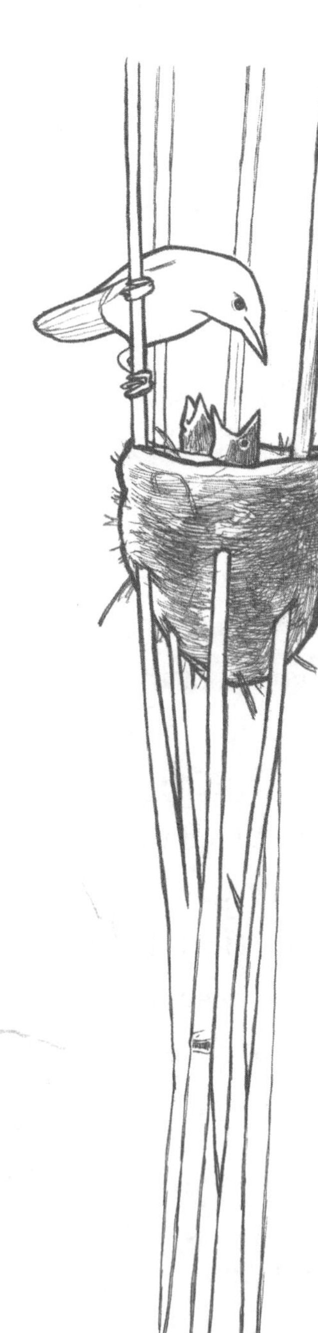

This strong nest will not fall down, even on a very windy day. Foxes that eat eggs and young chicks can't reach this nest. They can't walk in the swamp.

Polar bears hollow out a cozy den in a snowdrift. They often make an extra area as a playroom for the cubs. Snowstorms will cover the den's entrance, so the wise mother makes a breathing hole in the den's roof.

Female wolves dig a safe den underground. They make the entrance just large enough for their body, so no larger animal can enter. They often dig a ten-foot long tunnel that leads to a larger chamber where the mother will give birth.

In the Bible . . .

Did you know that Jesus is making a *perfect home* for you? Before Jesus died on the cross, He told His disciples, "There are many rooms in my Father's house. If this were not true, I would have told you. I am going there to prepare a place for you" (John 14:2;NIrV).

Can you imagine what kind of a home Jesus would prepare? Read what the apostle John saw in the "new heaven and new earth" (Revelation 21 and 22).

God is going to wipe away every tear from our eyes. There will be no more death, disappointments, sorrow, crying, or pain. There will be no more night. Our new home will be filled with the light of God. And it lasts forever. It's the PERFECT home!

How about you?

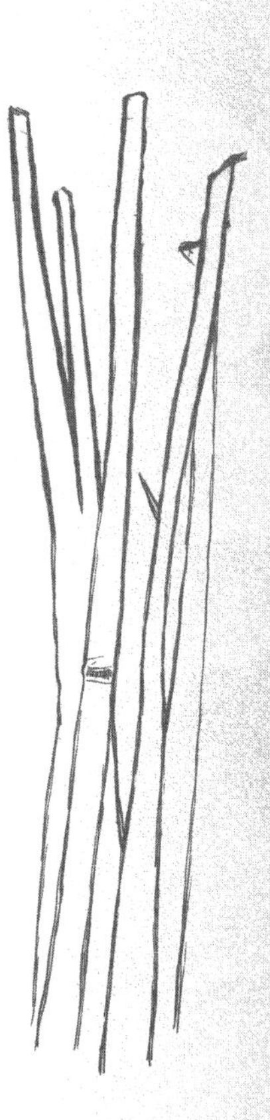

Imagine what a *perfect* home with Jesus would be like. What would it feel like to always be happy? What if you never felt sad, mad, or angry? Imagine a home where everyone loves God and each other. Imagine never going to bed!

If animals know how to make good homes for their babies, you can be sure that Jesus has made a *perfect* home for you. He knows what will make you very, very happy!

Memory Verse:

In My Father's house are many mansions
. . . I go to prepare a place for you.
(John 14:2)

Amazing Wings

Dragonflies spend most of their lives flying. They have two pairs of amazing wings that are *not* linked together. They flap independently. These large, fast-beating wings enable the dragonfly to hover like a helicopter, fly backward, or stop in an instant.

When the dragonfly hovers, the front pair of wings creates a downbeat, while the second pair of wings makes an upbeat. This amazing X-shaped fluttering enables the dragonfly to stop in mid-air as if hanging on an invisible string.

Can you imagine having six legs, but never using them to walk? The dragonfly's six legs are all located at the front of its body. The legs help catch insects in mid-air. Once in a while a dragonfly uses its legs to perch on a plant. But it *never* walks.

In the Bible . . .

Do you remember a beggar in the Bible who had never walked on his legs? He was lame from birth. Every day someone carried him to the temple gate where he sat and begged.

One day Peter and John saw him when they went up to the temple to pray. Peter said to him, "I don't have any silver or gold. But I'll give you what I have. In the name of Jesus Christ of Nazareth, get up and walk."

Peter took him by the hand and lifted him up. Immediately the man's feet and ankles were strong. He leaped up and entered the temple with them. But he didn't just *walk*. He joyfully jumped and leaped! He praised God with a loud voice! (Acts 3:1–10;NIrV).

How about you?

When is the last time that you thanked God for your legs? If you were sick or crippled, would you still thank God for all that He gives you?

Do you get excited about the many wonderful creatures God created? What are some of the interesting gifts God has given to you (like He gave the dragonfly its special wings)? Stop and think about your amazing mind and body. *You* are even more amazing than a dragonfly!

Memory Verse:

Know that the Lord, He is God; It is He who has made us, and not we ourselves.
(Psalm 100:4)

Watch That Tongue

Have you ever seen a snake flick its tongue? It does not use its tongue to inject poison into its victims. From the way a snake uses its tongue, it seems to be tasting.

Even though a snake's tongue doesn't have taste buds like ours, its tongue does help the snake to *taste* whatever chemicals are in the air around it.

A snake needs its tongue to help find food. If you lived down in the grass and rocks like a snake does, you'd be glad if your tongue picked up scents of small animals or birds for your next meal.

The two tips of its tongue help a snake follow the trail of its prey. Tasty chemicals brought in by the right fork and the left fork can differ. More taste on one side means that the trail of the prey is turning in that direction. If there are equal amounts of taste on both forks, that means the trail goes straight.

In the Bible . . .

The apostle James says a lot about our tongues. "The tongue is a small part of the body. But it brags a lot. Think about how a small spark can set a big forest on fire. The tongue also is a fire. . . . People have controlled [tamed] all kinds of animals . . . But no one can control the tongue. It is an evil thing that never rests. It is full of deadly poison. With our tongues we praise our Lord and Father. With our tongues we call down curses on people. . . . Praise and cursing come out of the same mouth. My brothers and sisters, it shouldn't be that way" (James 3:7-10;NIrV).

How about you?

Just as its tongue affects the path the snake takes, so your tongue affects your life. The words you speak will either take you closer or farther away from God.

Think about how you use your tongue. Do the words you speak bring blessing or hurt to others? Your tongue will always affect many people. Do you gossip? Do you tell lies? Have your words ever made someone cry?

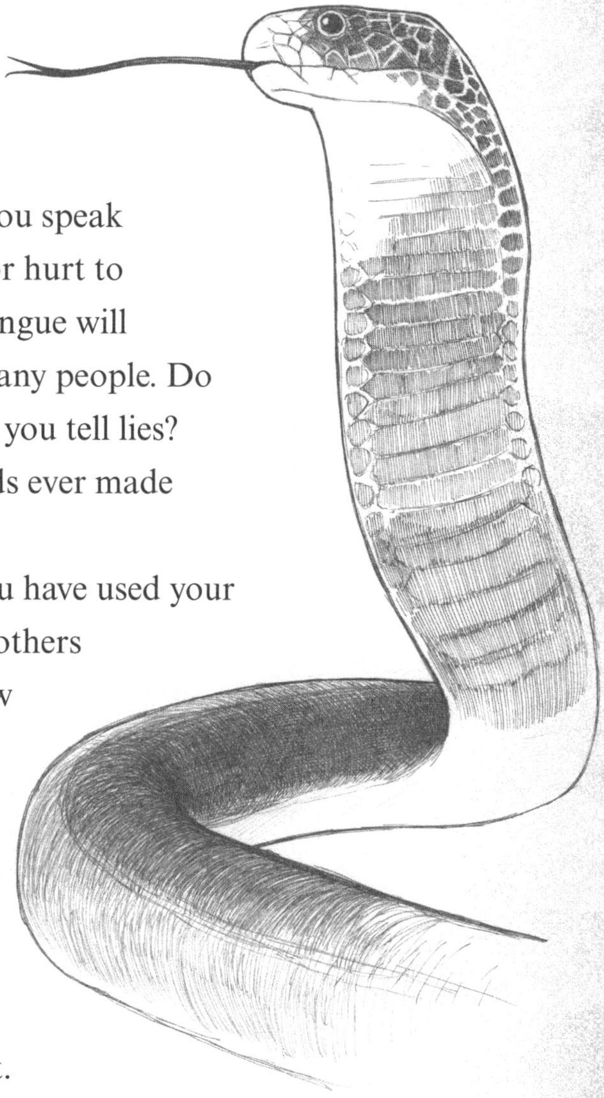

Perhaps you have used your tongue to hurt others in the past. Now use your tongue again — ask for forgiveness, from God and from the person you hurt.

Memory Verse:

"So get rid of every kind of evil. Stop telling lies . . . Don't speak against each other."
(1 Peter 2:1;NIrV)

Listen Carefully!

Grasshoppers do not have any ears on their heads. A grasshopper hears everything through a special membrane called a tympanum. The tympanum is found on the grasshopper's abdomen, just in front of each hind leg.

Male grasshoppers communicate through special chirping sounds. They rapidly drag the hard pegs of their large hind legs over their two front wings. This produces a unique pattern of chirps.

Each of the 23,000 species of Orthoptera (a large order of insects) has its own pattern of chirps!

If you sat outside in a field, you would hear lots of grasshoppers making sounds. But your ears could never pick out the different sound of each species.

Female grasshoppers can hear the slightest differences in the rhythm and tone of grasshopper sounds. And females will only respond to the calls made by males of their *own* species. That takes a special kind of careful listening!

In the Bible . . .

Can you remember some people in the Bible who heard God's voice? Samuel heard someone call his name when he was a young boy who lived in God's temple. He thought that Eli, the temple priest, had called him. He got out of bed and hurried to Eli's bedside and said, "Here I am."

"I didn't call you," said Eli. "Go back and lie down."

Samuel lay down in bed. He heard his name called again. So he went again to the priest. But Eli insisted that he had not called the boy.

When this happened the third time, Eli realized that God might be calling the boy. So he told Samuel to say, "Speak, Lord. I'm listening."

This was the first time God had spoken to a person in many years. God told Samuel that He would punish Eli and his sons. God was angry because Eli did not stop his sons from doing evil (1 Samuel 3:1–19;NIrV).

What about you?

Do you trust that God is speaking to you when you read your Bible? Do you ever listen for God to speak? Do you listen carefully when someone else reads the Bible? God has promised to bless those who *hear* His Word and *keep* it. God still speaks to His children today. Just like Samuel, you can learn to *hear* His voice.

Memory Verse:

Jesus said, "He who has ears to hear, let him hear!"
(Matthew 13:9)

The King of Cats

Most people think of the lion as the "king of the jungle." But the majestic Bengal tigers are the largest cats in the world. Their beautiful orange and black pattern of stripes makes them the most impressive big cat. Male tigers can stand as tall as 3 feet at their shoulders. They grow to be 13 feet long (including their tails).

The largest tigers weigh about 600 pounds. And each hungry cat eats 6,000 pounds of meat every year!

The Bengal tiger is also much stronger than almost any other animal — a crocodile, or a hippo, or even a rhinoceros. The tiger's sharp claws hold so tightly to its prey that nothing can escape from its strong and deadly grip. The handsome Bengal tiger is truly the KING of cats . . . and *all* wildlife.

In the Bible . . .

Outward looks and appearances never impress God. Once God told the prophet Samuel to anoint one of Jesse's sons to be the next king of Israel. When Samuel saw Eliab, the oldest son, he was sure that God would choose that tall, handsome young man to be king.

But God told Samuel, "Do not look at his appearance or at his physical stature, because I have refused him. For the Lord does not see as man sees; for man looks at the outward appearance, but the Lord looks at the heart" (1 Samuel 16:7).

Then God picked David, the smallest and youngest of Jesse's eight sons, to be the greatest king that ever ruled the people of Israel (1 Samuel 16:1–13).

What about you?

Are you impressed by what people look like? Do you think more of someone because of what they wear, what they own, or how they look? Remember what God looks at — the heart. God knows what we are thinking. God sees how we treat others. God is looking for people to trust and obey Him.

Are you willing to look at others (and yourself) the way God does? Try it today. Try to learn what someone is really like . . . not just what they *look like*. And remember that God has a big plan for you, even when you are still young.

Memory Verse:

For man looks at the outward appearance, but the Lord looks at the heart.
(1 Samuel 16:7)

A Wise Builder

The brush turkeys of Australia build some of the best nests. Year after year, they return to lay their eggs in the same nest.

When a female turkey gets ready to lay her first eggs, she builds a tall mound of twigs and leaves. Most nests are about four feet wide and three feet high. Some turkeys build nests that reach as high as ten feet!

When the pile of dead leaves decays, it heats the nest. That keeps the nest warm enough to hatch the eggs. The male turkey is the one who tests the temperature of the nest by pushing his head down in the leaves. He makes sure it is ready for the eggs. Then the female lays 7 to 12 eggs and buries them about two feet under the mound of leaves. Lots of insects, worms, and spiders will also make

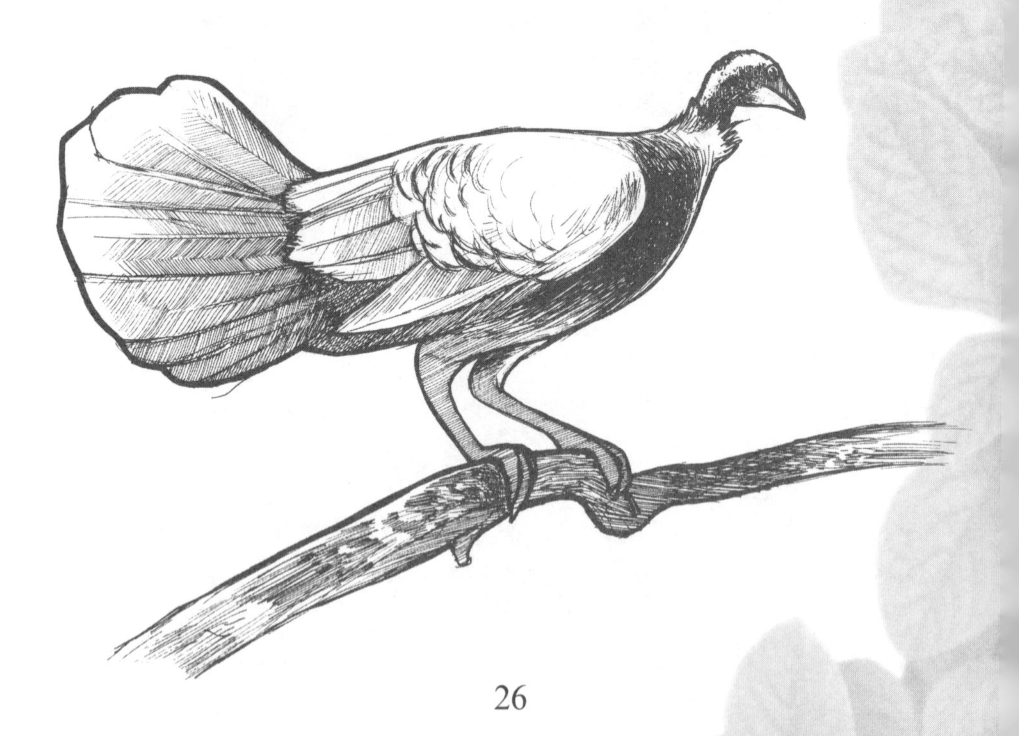

their homes inside the warm nest. When the baby turkeys are born, they will feed on these insects.

In the Bible . . .

Jesus cares about how we build our lives. He told this story: "Everyone who hears my words and puts them into practice is like a wise man. He builds his house on the rock. The rain comes down. The water rises. The winds blow and beat against that house. But it does not fall. It is built on the rock.

"But everyone who hears my words and does not put them into practice is like a foolish man. He builds his house on sand. The rain comes down. The water rises. The winds blow and beat against that house. And it falls with a loud crash" (Matthew 7:24–27;NIrV).

How about you?

How do you build your life on a rock? Jesus said that the wise builder was the one who heard God's words and *obeyed* them.

How often do you take time to read your Bible? Do you obey God's Word? When you feel worried, do you pray? Do you look for friends who do what is right? Do you obey your parents? Do you forgive others? When you do what God says, you are building your life on a firm foundation.

Memory Verse:

Dear friends, build yourselves up
in you most holy faith.
(Jude 1:20)

A Fearless Flier

The Chinese fly many kites. They invented the kite. But the first kite ever flown was by a young spider!

Have you ever seen a spider web hanging in between two bushes or between your roof and a nearby tree? How do these webs get started?

A spider that lives in a tree or in the eaves of a house makes a big leap of faith as it jumps out into the air while it is spinning its web. Even baby spiders that first come out of their egg sac often climb to the top of a blade of grass and face the wind. They lift up their backs and spin some tiny silken threads. These threads are so light that they float.

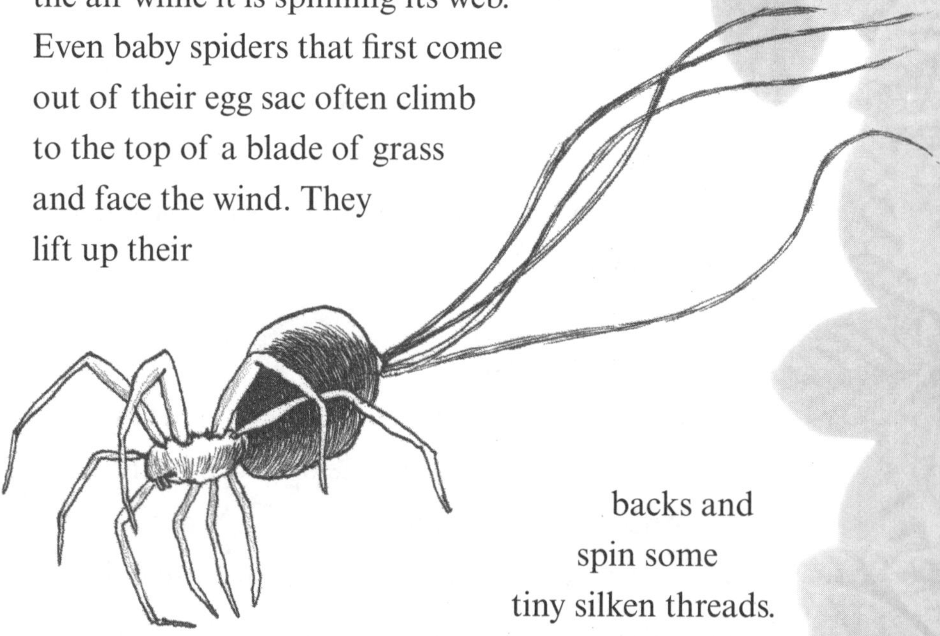

As the threads grow, the wind pulls on them. The baby spider hangs onto the grass while it spins the threads longer. Then it lets go of the grass and sails off like a kite into the sky! When the spider lands in a new place, it spins a web and begins a new life. Some spiders have been carried long distances on their silky kites. They have even landed on ships located hundreds of miles from shore.

In the Bible . . .

After Moses died, Joshua became the leader of the people of Israel. Can you imagine how Joshua felt? He knew they had to cross the flooded Jordan River. He knew they would have to fight the walled city of Jericho and many other cities.

Joshua must have felt afraid because God told him three times, "Be strong and very courageous" (Joshua 1:6, 7, 9).

God also promised Joshua, "As I was with Moses, so I will be with you. I will not leave you nor forsake you" (Joshua 1:5). Then Joshua trusted God. And God helped him conquer many enemies in the Promised Land.

How about you?

Where in your life do you need to trust God more? Do you ever feel afraid to try something new and different? Do you worry about what others will say? Are you afraid that you will fail? What scares you more than anything else does?

Is there a time when you have trusted God and done what was right, even when it was hard? God will help you conquer fear. He will make you bold and courageous!

Memory Verse:

Be strong and of good courage; do not be afraid, nor be dismayed, for the Lord your God is with you wherever you go.
(Joshua 1:9)

Struggles That Strengthen

Standing on a high rocky slope, a young mountain goat acts like he is king of the mountain. Suddenly, another young goat climbs up the rocks and leaps at him. Both goats rise up on their hind legs. They clash horns. Their battle continues as they lock horns. They push head against head, neither willing to give up. The sharp edges of their hooves dig into the rocky hillside.

At first, this battle seems to be a fight to the death, enemy against enemy. But this battle is not a war of two strangers. It is a contest of young friends. The goats actually compete like this against each other all day, every day.

These contests are done for sport. They are usually between young goats of the same size and strength. This struggle will help both of the goats increase in strength, balance, and skill.

In the Bible . . .

"Jesus, full of the Holy Spirit, returned from the Jordan River. The Spirit led him into the desert. There the devil tempted him for 40 days. Jesus ate nothing during that time. At the end of the 40 days, he was hungry" (Luke 4:1–2).

When Jesus was weak and hungry, the devil came to tempt Him. But Jesus stood strong against the devil and the devil finally left. Afterwards, God's angels came to strengthen Jesus. And Jesus returned home with new strength "in the power of the Holy Spirit." At this time Jesus began His miracle-working ministry.

How about you?

What do you do when life gets tough? Hard times and struggles often end up making us wiser and stronger.

Remember the mountain goats. Their struggles make them stronger. Think of a time when you struggled with homework, or with someone who was teasing you. Did you grow closer to God and others during that time?

Remember how Jesus also suffered and struggled. He understands how you feel when you face tough times. He will strengthen you in every difficulty.

Memory Verse:

Blessed is the man who endures trial, for when he has stood the test he will receive the crown of life which God has promised to those who love Him.
(James 1:12)

FIGHT . . . OR MAKE PEACE

Here's a riddle: What do you get when you cross a deer and an insect? It's the stag beetle.

The male stag beetles are most famous for the large, hard "antlers" called mandibles. These antlers stick out of the sides of their mouths.

These powerful antler-horns are used for fierce battles, especially when the beetles compete for a mate, food, or territory.

The females are no weaklings either. Although their horns are much smaller, they are also very strong.

Beetles are found all over the world. One female produces 30-70 eggs per season. Stag beetles feed on rotting wood. Look for them under stones, logs, or fallen leaves in your own backyard.

Maybe you'll even see two males fighting over the same mate.

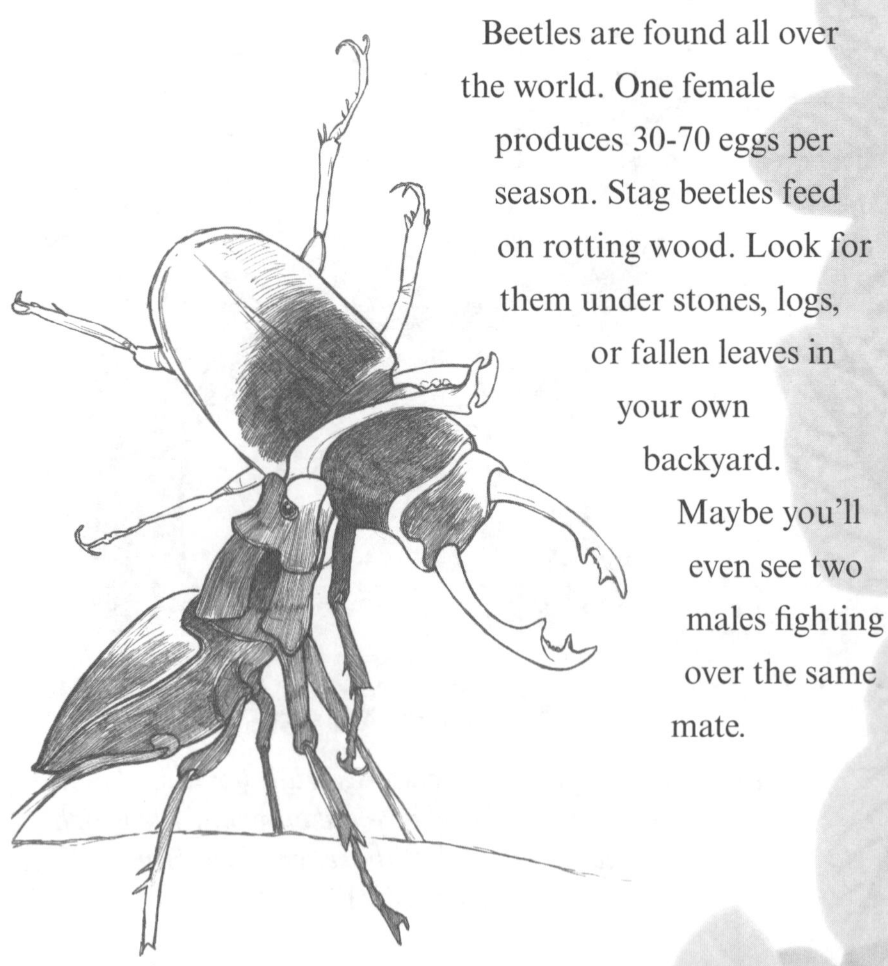

In the Bible . . .

Long ago, two women in the Bible fought over a baby (1 Kings 3:16-28). They each gave birth to a baby boy. When one baby died during the night, his mother switched him with the other living baby. The other mother woke up and argued, "The living baby is my son! The dead baby is yours."

They came to King Solomon. He wanted to find out who the real mother was, so he said, "Bring me a sword." He told his soldiers, "Divide the living child in two. Give half to one woman and half to the other."

"Don't kill him!" one mother cried. "Give him to the other woman."

But the other woman said, "Go ahead and divide him."

Then King Solomon knew who the real mother was. He told his soldiers, "Don't kill the child. Give him to the first woman. She is his mother."

How about you?

In the world of nature, there is much fighting among animals. Even among people, hatred and jealousy leads to fights. Will you be a peacemaker? Will you be like the mother who was willing to let the other woman have her baby so that he might live? Write down one way that you can make peace in your home today.

Memory Verse:

Jesus said, "Blessed are the peacemakers, for they shall be called sons of God."
(Matthew 5:9)

Grace and Beauty

What is the most elegant and graceful member of the antelope family? It is the gazelle. The gazelle's small, ringed horns sit above a pair of large, soft eyes. Its pointed ears have a keen sense of hearing.

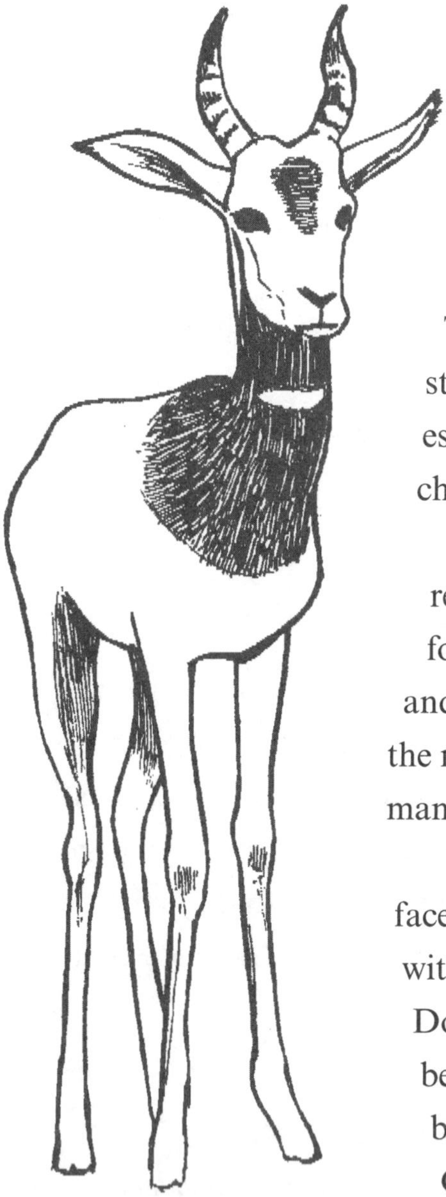

The legs of a gazelle are long and slender. On each knee there is a small tuft of hair. They zigzag back and forth when they run away from predators. Their energy and great stamina often helps them escape an attacking lion or cheetah.

The tallest gazelles only reach between three and four feet. Its slender form and long legs make it one of the most graceful small mammals in the world.

In the middle of its lovely face, the gazelle is marked with a triangle-shaped streak. Doesn't the gazelle look beautiful? When we see its beauty, we should thank God for His wonderful world.

In the Bible . . .

Ruth came to Bethlehem with her mother-in-law, Naomi. Both Ruth and Naomi were poor widows. Ruth went to the fields to find food for herself and Naomi. She worked hard gathering leftover grain for them to eat.

Boaz, the rich owner of the fields, saw Ruth working in his field. He found out how much she helped her mother-in-law. So he told his workers to give her extra grain. Later Boaz, who greatly admired Ruth, took her to be his wife.

We don't know if Ruth looked beautiful. We do know that everyone in Bethlehem said that Ruth was thoughtful, kind, and generous. Her beautiful spirit of giving and serving caused others to love and admire her. Other women told Naomi, "Your daughter-in-law, who loves you . . . is better to you than seven sons" (Ruth 4:15).

How about you?

Gazelles look beautiful, Ruth had a great inner beauty, and guess what? *You* are also beautiful! Everything that God created is beautiful in a unique way.

Yet the most important beauty to God is the beauty of your heart. Ask Jesus to come into your heart and make you into a kind, loving, and beautiful person. Let Jesus give you a heart that loves other people.

Memory Verse:

He has made everything beautiful in its time.
(Ecclesiastes 3:11)

A Deep Voice

The bullfrog is the largest frog in America. The bullfrog is most famous for its deep voice. Some say that a bullfrog's voice sounds like the bellow of a faraway bull.

You will hear the frogs' deep, bass tones in the spring after they come out from the mud where they hibernate through the winter. By mid-summer, their voices grow louder. The frogs join together in a nightly chorus that is heard in swamps, lakes, and streams.

Bullfrogs hear each other with special "ears." Their ears are the large circles on the outside of their head and behind their eyes. These circles are made up of thin membranes which vibrate when sound waves hit them.

This greenish-brown frog grows to eight inches long. The bullfrog's powerful hinds legs often measure ten inches long. These legs make the bullfrog a great jumper and swimmer.

In the Bible . . .

The apostle Paul and his friend Silas were whipped and put into prison. Instead of feeling sorry for themselves, they prayed and sang to God.

Then a great earthquake shook the prison. The doors of the prison broke open and everyone's chains fell off! Once the jailer saw the prison doors open, he thought the prisoners had fled. He knew that he would be punished if they escaped. He got out his sword and was going to kill himself.

Paul called to him, "Do yourself no harm, for we are all here." Paul told the jailer and his family about Jesus. Then Paul baptized all of them (Acts 16:16–34).

How about you?

How often do you use your voice to praise God or sing to Him? Do you praise God when you wake up in the morning? Do you praise him for your family and for the work you have to do? Will you also praise God during times of trouble?

Praising God shows that you trust him and that you want to serve him, no matter what happens. Sing a new song to God today. Sing a song that has never been sung before. Make up your own words and your own tune.

Or praise God by putting new words to your favorite old tune. Praise God, even if you can't sing as well as a bullfrog!

Memory Verse:

Oh, sing to the Lord a new song! Sing to the Lord, all the earth.
(Psalm 96:1)

Dead . . . or Alive?

Don't throw away that dry, dead-looking leaf! It might be a cocoon.

A dull, brown cocoon only *looks* like it is dead. It is protecting something inside that's alive. The caterpillar that wrapped itself up in the cocoon is being totally changed.

It doesn't take long before the dead-looking cocoon cracks open at one end. Something inside is pushing on the shell. Finally it breaks through the split in the end.

Now watch carefully. A small, black head and two antennae poke out. Soon a long body with six legs and two folded wings will crawl from the opening.

The new creature patiently rests to gain strength. Finally it slowly stretches out its wrinkled wings and dries them in the sun.

What a *resurrection*! The caterpillar that could only crawl short distances on its stubby legs, now gets ready to fly! A big change happened inside of its "grave." A beautiful butterfly will fly up in the sky to live a new life.

In the Bible . . .

When their brother Lazarus became ill, Mary and Martha sent for Jesus. Instead of hurrying to their home, Jesus waited until Lazarus died.

When Jesus did go to see Martha, Lazarus had been dead four days. Jesus told Martha, "Your brother will rise again. . . . I am the resurrection and the life. He who believes in Me, though he may die, he shall live."

Then Jesus went to Lazarus' grave in the hillside. He said, "Take away the stone." After the men rolled away the stone from the grave's opening, Jesus cried with a loud voice, "Lazarus, come forth!"

Lazarus came out alive! Jesus showed His power over death! (John 11:1–44).

What about you?

Have you ever been to a funeral of someone you loved? Can you picture them in Heaven with Jesus, alive and well?

When you trust Jesus as your Savior and Lord, you can be sure He will give you a new life when you die. And God will give you a new resurrected body. It will be a body that never gets sick or feels tired. Your body will be raised in glory and power. (Read 1 Corinthians 15:35-58.) Even now Jesus is already changing you here on earth. He is making you more like Him every day.

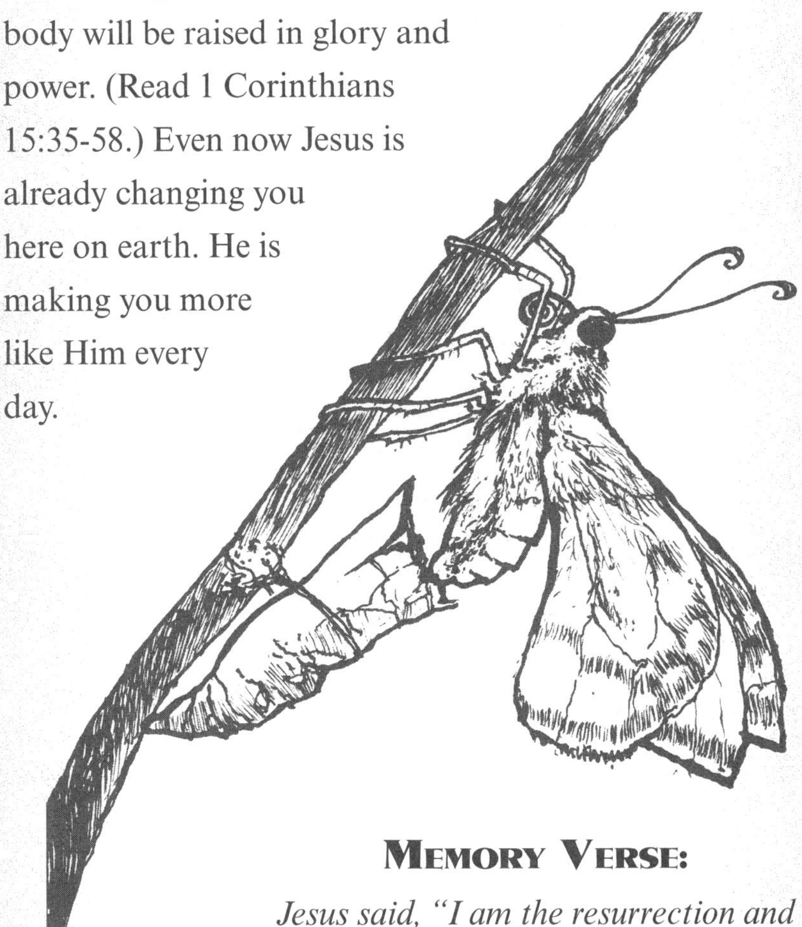

Memory Verse:

Jesus said, "I am the resurrection and the life. He who believes in Me, though he may die, he shall live."
(John 11:25)

The "Blind" See

Whoever made up the phrase, "blind as a bat," did not understand that bats are not blind. Fruit bats use their keen eyesight and sense of smell to find food at night. But insect-eating bats use a form of "animal radar" to find their way around in the dark. These bats don't have to use their eyes to see where they are going. Instead, they send out sonar signals. A bat makes these signals by squeezing its throat muscles. The high-pitched signals then fly out into the air through the bat's nose.

Those same signals bounce off an insect and bounce back to the bat's super-sensitive ears. The bat flies towards the insect by following its returning sonar signals.

Bats know how far away an object is based on how long it takes for the sonar signals to come back to them. It seems like other signals sent out by bat neighbors would confuse a bat. But every bat knows which returning sonar signals belong to it.

Bats help many farmers. They eat tons of insects that would harm farm crops and ruin fruit trees. And it all happens when the bats "see" in the dark!

In the Bible . . .

"As Jesus went along, he saw a man who was blind. He had been blind since he was born. . . .

"[Jesus] spit on the ground. He made some mud with the spit. Then he put the mud on the man's eyes.

"Go," [Jesus] told him. "Wash in the Pool of Siloam." . . . So the man went and washed. And he came home able to see" (John 9:1–8;NIrV).

Blindness was never a problem for Jesus to heal. In fact, Jesus called himself the *Light of the World*. And He promised, "Those who follow me will never walk in darkness" (John 8:12;NIrV).

How about you?

Jesus is the Creator who gave bats their ability to "see." Jesus healed the blind man. And Jesus helps you "see" Him and believe in Him today (even when you cannot see Him with your physical eyes).

Jesus will help you "see" how you can be a blessing to many people, just like bats are helpful to many farmers. Keep close to Jesus as you pray, read His Word, and live for Him. He will help you "see" where you are going. He is your light.

Memory Verse:

Jesus said, "I am the light of the world.
He who follows Me shall not walk in
darkness, but have the light of life."
(John 8:12)

The Potter Provides

The potter wasp gets its name from the way it builds its nest out of mud. The wasp works a lot like a potter who shapes a pot out of clay.

The potter wasp uses her jaws to carry water from puddles to her nest. She uses her front legs to shape the mud mixture into balls. Then she stacks the mud balls together to form the round wall of her pot. Can you imagine how many trips the wasp makes to carry water before the mud home for her eggs is completed?

When the pot is finished, she forms a neat little lip at the top. Then the wasp backs up into the pot opening and lays her eggs. She hangs her sac of eggs by a silk thread from the pot's ceiling.

The mother also knows that when her baby larvae hatch they will need lots of food. So she lightly paralyzes some caterpillars and puts them in the pot. When the babies hatch they will have a supply of food to keep them alive.

In the Bible . . .

Just like the potter wasp has a curious way of protecting her children, so our God has curious ways of protecting us and providing for us.

God sent the prophet Elijah to a widow during a time of famine. Elijah asked the widow to fix him a meal. The woman told Elijah that she and her son had only a little bit of oil and flour left. She was getting ready to bake their last meal.

Elijah told her not to worry. He promised that God would never let her oil or flour run out IF she fed

Elijah first. So the widow used the last of her oil and flour to feed Elijah. And God kept His promise. The oil and flour never ran out during the time of famine (1 Kings 17:8–16).

How about you?

Do you ever worry about problems in your life? Do you worry about things that *might* happen to you? Did you know that it is wrong to worry? Worry shows that you aren't sure if God will help you or take good care of you.

Remember: God makes insects that take good care of their babies. God fed a poor widow and her son. Don't you think God knows how to take care of you? He is the master potter. What in your life today do you need to trust God to provide?

Memory Verse:

O Lord, You are our Father; we are the clay, and You our potter; And all we are the work of Your hand.
(Isaiah 64:8)

Need for Speed

Have you ever seen a jack rabbit run through a field? Take a close look at the rabbit's long hind legs. These strong legs enable a rabbit to run at speeds of up to 50 miles per hour over short distances.

The 30 species of jack rabbits all have black tips on their ears. They are faster and more powerful runners than other rabbits. Why does the jack rabbit run so fast? Why does he need such speed?

In the open and treeless plains with no place to hide, the ability to run with great speed is important. Rabbits have no means of defense. Adult jack rabbits have long been famous for their quick get-away from larger predators, such as wolves, owls, and foxes.

As with most living things, the jack rabbit's body, especially its long ears and strong hind legs, is equipped to help it stay ALIVE!

In the Bible . . .

There are many stories in the Bible where God gave His people just what they needed. Think of the time when Elijah prayed for rain on the top of Mount Carmel.

When the servant reported that he saw a small cloud coming up over the sea, Elijah said, "Go to Ahab [the king]. Tell him, 'Tie your chariot to your horse. Go down to Jezreel before the rain stops you.' "

"Black clouds filled the sky. The wind came up, and a heavy rain began to fall. Ahab rode off to Jezreel.

"The power of the Lord came on Elijah. He tucked his coat into his belt. And he ran ahead of Ahab all the way to Jezreel" (1 Kings 18:41–46;NIrV).

How about you?

Do you trust that God will give you what you need when you need it? You may not need speed to run like a rabbit. You may not need speed to run like Elijah when he had to race ahead of the storm. But God knows exactly what you do need.

God knows when you need food and clothes. God knows when you need a friend. God knows when you need help during times of trouble. God even knows what you need *before* you ask. Take all your needs to Him in prayer.

Memory Verse:

Your Father knows the things you have need of before you ask Him.
(Matthew 6:8)

One Body

On warm oceans around the world, you may see a blue jelly-like balloon, bobbing atop the waves. It can be as wide as six feet! It moves as it is pushed by the wind. But beware! Do not be fooled. What you see is one of the sea's most feared predators. It is called the Portuguese man-of-war. Many stinging tentacles, some as long as 60 feet, hang down under its balloon top. Their painful stings can paralyze large fish and also seriously injure a human swimmer.

The Portuguese man-of-war *looks* like it is a single, large creature. But it is made up of many small groups called polyps. All of these living groups are attached to the main stem. They work and cooperate together to make the jellyfish seem like one single creature.

The man-of-war could never live without this cooperation. Once its prey is paralyzed by the stinging polyps, many of the feeding polyps slowly digest the meal. The nutrition is shared among the whole body.

In the Bible . . .

Just as many different organisms make up the man-of-war, so many different Christians are "attached" to Jesus. When we are one with Jesus, we become part of the body of Christ. The apostle Paul wrote, "There is one body. But it has many members. Even though it has many parts, they make up one body. It is the same with Christ. We were all baptized by one Holy Spirit into one body. . . . Suppose the foot says, 'I am not a hand. So I don't belong to the body.' It is still part of the body.

"And suppose the ear says, 'I am not an eye. So I don't

belong to the body.' It is still part of the body. If the whole body were an eye, how could it hear? If the whole body were an ear, how could it smell?

"God has placed each part in the body just as he wanted it to be. . . . As it is, there are many parts. But there is only one body" (1 Corinthians 12:12–20).

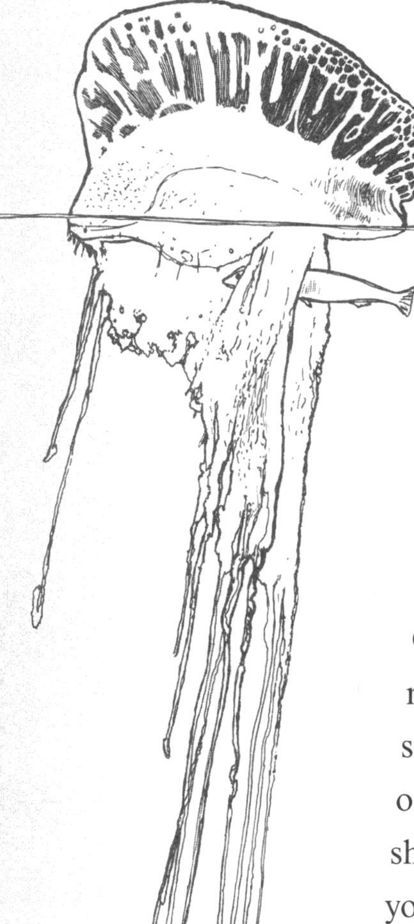

How about you?

Do you trust in Jesus as your Savior and Lord? Then you belong to the body of Christ. You are important, no matter how young or how short you are. Every member of Christ's Body has a gift to share and a job to do. What is your gift? What is one job you can do to bless other people in the body of Christ?

Memory Verse:

But now God has set the members, each one of them, in the body just as He pleased.
(1 Corinthians 12:18)

A Powerful Bird of Prey

The raptors are known as birds of prey. A "bird of prey" gets most of its food by hunting other animals.

Using its powerful wings, a raptor swoops down from the sky in the blink of an eye. Pouncing on its prey, the raptor uses its strong feet, powerful beak, and razor-sharp talons to capture and hang on to its prey.

This raptor is called a Northern Goshawk. It lives in the forests of Europe and North America. Its long tail and shorter, rounded wings help the goshawk make quick turns to catch its prey.

Without its power, speed, and a strong body built for hunting, the raptor would be unable to feed itself or its young. But God knew exactly what the Northern Goshawk needed.

In the Bible . . .

The prophet Elijah challenged the prophets of Baal to show whose God was the greatest and most powerful. He said, "You pray to your gods, and I'll pray to the Lord. The god who answers by sending fire down is the one and only God."

The prophets of Baal set up an altar with a bull on top. They prayed all day to Baal. They even cut themselves with knives. But Baal never answered.

Then Elijah built an altar with 12 stones. He placed a bull and some wood on top of it. He also dug a trench around the altar. Then he had 12 pots full of water poured over the altar. Water ran down the altar and filled up the trench.

Then Elijah prayed to God. Immediately God showed His power. Fire came down! It burned up everything. It even burned the stones and the trench full of water! All of the people fell on their faces and cried, "The Lord is the one and only God!" (1 Kings 18:20–39;NIrV).

How about you?

Do you ever think that your problems are too big for God? The strength of the goshawk is only a small reflection of the power of God. Where do you need God's power and help today? Ask, and God will show you His power and strength. If you are God's child, God will answer you, just like He answered Elijah.

Memory Verse:

[God] gives power to the faint, and to him who has no might he increases strength.
(Isaiah 40:29)

Tiny, but Spiny

The brook stickleback is only two-and-a-half inches long. It lives in the cool, clear brooks of the eastern United States.

The stickleback is tiny, but it is very brave. It will fight larger fish. It uses its teeth and pointed spines to attack its opponent. Sometimes male sticklebacks even fight each other to the death!

A male stickleback builds a special nest. Using glue-like threads that come out a special gland, he pastes water plants together (like a spider forms its web).

Once his nest is built, the male stickleback drives a female inside. After she lays as many as 100 eggs, he then takes over the care of the eggs. This faithful father fish will stay with the nest and take care of the eggs. Later, this brave little fish will also protect his newly hatched babies from any enemies.

In the Bible . . .

The angel of the Lord said to Gideon, "Mighty warrior, the Lord is with you." But Gideon was not a brave man or a "mighty" man. Gideon was scared.

God told Gideon, "You are strong. Go and save Israel from the power of Midian. I am sending you. . . . I will be with you."

Gideon said, "But Lord, how can I possibly save Israel. My family group is the weakest . . . And I am the least important member of my family." Gideon finally did what God asked him to do. And God helped him be a brave leader who won victory over the enemy (Judges 6:12–16;NIrV).

How about you?

Do you ever get picked on because you are small? Remember the stickleback's bravery. That little fish fights off larger fish as he defends his young. He is a brave father as well as a clever nest builder.

Do you ever feel scared like Gideon? Remember why Gideon ended up being a brave leader — he did what God told him, even when he felt scared. Ask for God's help when you feel weak or fearful.

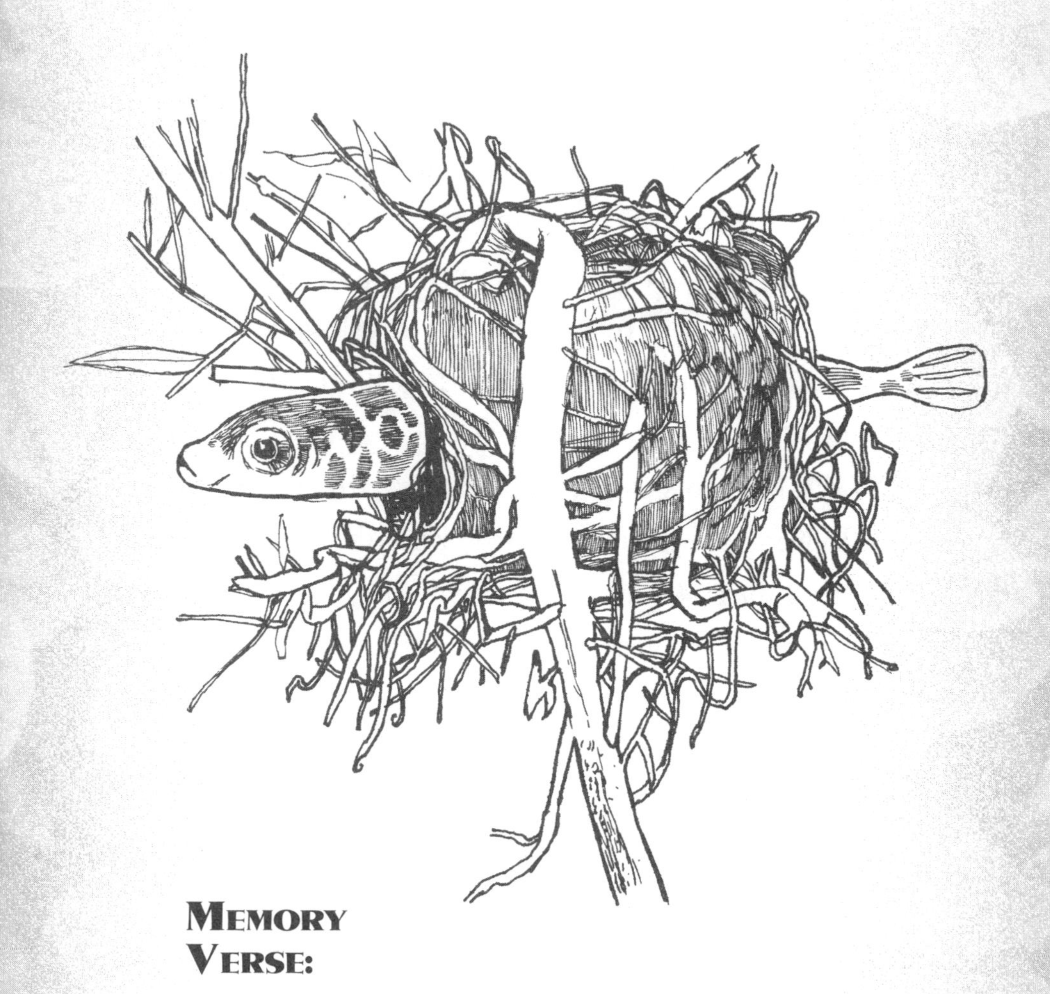

Memory Verse:

Fear not, for I am with you . . . I am your God. I will strengthen you. Yes, I will help you. (Isaiah 41:10)

Listen for the Shepherd

Sheep are some of the most helpless of all animals. Sheep need a shepherd! Except for the rams with horns, most sheep can't do much to defend themselves. They can't even run fast.

Sheep are also known for being stupid. They can never find their way to green pastures or quiet streams. When left alone, they will ruin and trample pastures. When they are thirsty, they drink from dirty puddles and often get sick.

A shepherd must keep close watch over his flock. Sheep get lost easily. They often go astray. If a sheep is missing, the shepherd searches for it immediately. If a sheep has fallen down and turned over on its back, it needs help fast. It can't get back up by itself. It will quickly die in the hot sun.

Even though sheep are so helpless, there is one thing they do well. They know their shepherd's voice. Strangers can't trick them. Even if someone looks like the shepherd, they still have a different voice. And the sheep know their shepherd's voice. When their shepherd calls, they follow.

In the Bible . . .

We are like sheep. And Jesus said, "The sheep listen to [the shepherd's] voice. He calls his own sheep by name and leads them out. When he has brought all of his own sheep out, he goes on ahead of them. His sheep follow him because they know his voice. They don't recognize a stranger's voice.

"I am the good shepherd. The good shepherd gives his life for the sheep. . . . My sheep listen to my voice. I know them, and they follow me. I give them eternal life, and they will never die. No one can steal them out of my hand" (John 10:3–28;NIrV).

Jesus bought you, His lamb, for a price — His life. He is *your* shepherd.

What about you?

Can you tell when Jesus speaks to you? When other people want you to join in doing something wrong, can you hear Jesus call you to follow Him?

Remember that Jesus speaks to you in His Word, the Bible. So listen to your Good Shepherd by reading your Bible each day. Listen to those who teach God's Word. Trust that Jesus will help you know when He is speaking to you.

Memory Verse:

Jesus said, "My sheep hear My voice, and I know them, and they follow Me."
(John 10:27)

Slow Down!

Green turtles lead a slow, easy-going life. These sea turtles often fall asleep as they float along the south Atlantic Ocean coastline. They wake up to feed mostly on seaweed along the coast. Turtles have lungs, so they must surface to breathe.

This turtle gets its name from the green color of its body fat. Its body is well built for life in the ocean. The turtle's smooth, flat shell allows it to swim easily through the ocean. Its large front legs work like paddles. They "row" gracefully in the water. But a green turtle is slow and clumsy when it walks on land.

Female turtles crawl up to the sand dunes above high tide and lay their eggs. A single female may lay several hundred eggs. Then she takes a different path back to the water. That helps keep predators from finding her new nest.

In the Bible . . .

"Jesus came to a village where a woman named Martha lived. She welcomed him into her home. She had a sister named Mary.

"Mary sat at the Lord's feet listening to what he said. But Martha was busy with all the things that had to be done. She came to Jesus and said, 'Lord, my sister has left me to do the work by myself. Don't you care? Tell her to help me!'

" 'Martha, Martha,' the Lord answered. 'You are worried and upset about many things. But only one thing is needed. Mary has chosen what is better. And it will not be taken away from her' " (Luke 10:38–42;NIrV).

How about you?

Think how good it feels to relax outside in the sunshine. Do you spend enough time just soaking in the words and wisdom of the Bible? Do you enjoy reading God's Word? Jesus knows how busy you are. He knows how easily you get upset and worried. He told Martha, "Only one thing is needed."

Will you follow Mary's example? Stop everything. Do the one thing that is important. Slow down, relax, and talk to Jesus. Seek first God's kingdom. Take a hint from the green turtle — relax in some of Jesus' *Son*-light.

Memory Verse:

Seek first the kingdom of God and His righteousness.
(Matthew 6:33)

Where's the Map?

Some people always get lost . . . even with a map! But how do the eastern monarch butterflies get directions for their long trip to Mexico?

Every fall the monarchs in the eastern United States and Canada fly south. They travel up to 2,500 miles (4,000 km) across cities, mountains, deserts, and valleys. They come from many different places. But they all end up in the same place: a wooded slope in the Sierra Madre in Mexico.

Believe it or not, the butterflies arrive on the same day in November. They cover the branches and trunks of every tree. More than 14 million butterflies have been seen in that wooded 20 acres.

What makes this trip so amazing is that these butterflies have never been to this place before. They will mate before they return north in the early spring. Then they will lay their eggs and die. Their offspring will make the same trip back to Mexico in the fall . . . without having ever been there!

In the Bible . . .

God knows how to lead people (as well as butterflies) in the right path. Once God sent a cloud by day and a pillar of fire by night to lead the people of Israel through the wilderness. As long as the people followed the cloud and the fire, they knew they were going in the right direction (Exodus 13:12).

Jesus picked 12 men to be His disciples. He told them, "Follow Me" (Mark 1:17). Jesus also said, "***I*** am the way, the truth, and the life. No one comes to the Father except through Me" (John 14:6). Follow Jesus. He knows the way to go.

How about you?

We all need someone to lead us in the right direction. Are you willing to *follow* Jesus? Will you let Him lead and guide you? Will you trust Him and not be afraid of the future? Will you walk close to Him when times get tough?

If God gives millions of butterflies their directions, you can be sure that God will lead you each day of your life. *You* are more precious to God than all the butterflies in the world!

Memory Verse:

I will instruct you and teach you
in the way you should go;
I will guide you with My eye.
(Psalm 32:8)

FRIENDS FOREVER

Compared to all other birds, parrots are friendly and very social. These colorful birds usually stick together in pairs. When they fly to their feeding grounds, they often fly so close that their wings almost touch.

If one parrot finds food, its excited calls bring the rest of the flock.

Parrots are very affectionate. They love being petted or stroked on their necks.

They keep each other company by "talking" or screeching back and forth. They are the best "talkers" in the animal kingdom and the most human of all birds.

Parrots seem to be able to learn rapidly. Pet parrots mimic sounds and words that they hear often, like a ringing telephone, parts of a song, and words like "pretty boy" and "talk to me."

When parrots aren't using their big beaks for chatting with friends, they use their beaks to crack hard-shelled nuts or to eat fruit.

IN THE BIBLE . . .

The most famous of all the friendships in the Bible is that of Jonathan and David. Jonathan loved David just as much as he loved himself.

Jonathan was generous to David. "Jonathan took off the robe he was wearing and gave it to David. He also gave him his military clothes. He even gave him his sword, his bow and his belt" (1 Samuel 18:4;NIrV).

Jonathan's father, King Saul, felt jealous of David. He planned to kill David. But Jonathan went to David and warned him to escape. And Jonathan promised to remain friends with David forever (1 Samuel 20:1–42).

Years later, when David became king, he still remembered Jonathan. And David gave Jonathan's crippled son a special home (2 Samuel 9:1–13).

How about you?

Do you have any friends who are generous like Jonathan? Are you a loyal and loving friend to others? Think of ways you could be a better friend this week.

Do you need a good friend? Then try your best to *be* a good friend. And remember the *Friend* who loves you and never gives up on you.

Memory Verse:

A friend loves at all times.
(Proverbs 17:17)

"Bee" What You Can Be

How does a bumblebee fly? Its small wings shouldn't be able to lift up its heavy body.

Only recently scientists learned how bumblebees fly: they warm up their muscles. The bumblebee controls its temperature by shivering its thorax muscles to warm them. So if the bumblebee's load is too heavy, it will build and generates more strength by shivering and warming itself.

Hold your arms out like airplane wings. Try to move them by using only the muscles in your chest and back (not your shoulders or arms). Bumblebees do this nearly 200 times per second when they fly!

A bumblebee cannot fly like a honeybee. They can't dart in circles and zoom quickly to the hive. The bumblebee is more clumsy and bulky in flight. (Watch one buzzing around your flowers.)

What if bumblebees quit flying because they were clumsy? Then the one special job — that only *they* can do — would never get done. They are the only bees with long enough tongues to pollinate the deep red clover blossoms!

In the Bible . . .

Many ordinary people that God picked for important jobs knew that they weren't as strong or wise as other people.

When God spoke to Moses from the burning bush, Moses felt he couldn't do the job God asked him to do.

"Who am I to go to the king and lead your people out of Egypt?" Moses said to God. "I have never been a good speaker. I wasn't one before you spoke to me and I'm not one now. I am slow at speaking and I can never think of what to say."

God promised to help Moses and to be with him. So, finally Moses accepted his assignment, even though he felt he couldn't do it. And with God's help, he led two million people out of Egypt (Exodus 3:1–4:17).

How about you?

When have *you* felt awkward and clumsy? Maybe you feel like you can't catch a ball or draw a picture very well. Do you compare yourself to others? Do you ever *stop* doing something because you think others do it better?

Ask God to show you what *YOUR* special job is in this world — then *DO IT!* Be brave. God will help you just as He has helped bumblebees and Moses.

Memory Verse:

I can do all things through Christ
who strengthens me.
(Philippians 4:13)

Shout It Out!

During the day these small, slender apes are usually quiet, but during sunrise and sunset, the gibbons howl and shout.

They live in small family groups made up of a pair and three or four offspring of various ages. The males strongly defend their territory by screaming and yelling. Even though their voices sound fierce, they seldom fight. Their voices are extra loud because each male gibbon has a throat sac that amplifies their shouts.

Among the apes, the gibbons are the most agile. This acrobatic ape travels for hours through the treetops without getting tired. They swing rapidly between branches that are sometimes 18 feet apart. Their extremely long arms and large hands help them grab one branch and reach for the next with the other hand.

Gibbons spend most of their time in the trees. When on the ground, they walk completely upright like a human. Their long arms reach all the way down to their toes.

In the Bible . . .

God must like noise. He gave animals the ability to roar, bark, yelp, holler, and squeal. Some animal sounds are too high and too low for humans to hear.

When people in the Bible praised God, they did it LOUDLY!

"Sing a new song to the Lord. He has done wonderful things . . . Shout to the Lord with joy, everyone on earth. Burst into joyful songs and make music . . . with the harp. Blow the trumpets. Give a blast on the ram's horn. Shout to the Lord with joy. He is the King. Let the ocean and everything in it roar. Let the world and all who live in it shout. Let the rivers clap their hands. Let the mountains sing together with joy. Let them sing to the Lord" (Psalm 98:1–8;NIrV).

What about you?

Think about how excited people get at a soccer or basketball game. They shout, holler, and yell. They jump up and down when their team wins.

Have you ever shouted with joy to the Lord? Why not? Think of what He has done for you. Take time to shout and make music to the Lord.

Memory Verse:

Praise the Lord! Praise Him with the sound of the trumpet . . . with dance . . . with loud cymbals; Praise Him with clashing cymbals! Let everything that has breath . . . praise the Lord!
(Psalm 150:1–6)

The Smallest Jewel

Hummingbirds are the smallest . . . and the most beautiful birds in the world. The Bee Hummingbird is a colorful "jewel" with its bright red, blue, and white feathers. It is about two and one-half inches long. It weighs less than one-tenth of an ounce. Its resting heartbeat is as high as 1,000 beats per minute! Because of its small size and the quiet hum from its wings, a Bee Hummingbird sounds and looks like a bee in flight.

All hummingbirds can move their wings in any direction. They fly forward and backward with amazing speed. You can only see a blur when their wings beat from 30 to 80 times per second! (How many times can you twirl a finger in a circle during one second?)

A hummingbird can reach into small, tightly closed flowers with its narrow, curved beak. It uses its long, powerful tongue to feed on nectar and tiny bugs found in flower blossoms.

Speed helps these small birds feed without ever landing. And they are so agile that they can pick a spider right out of its web!

In the Bible . . .

Jesus told a crowd of people, "Aren't five sparrows sold for two pennies? But God does not forget even one of them. In fact, he even counts every hair on your head! So don't be afraid. You are worth more than many sparrows. . . ."

"Don't worry about your life and what you will eat. And don't worry about your body and what you will wear . . . Think about the ravens. They don't plant or gather crops. They don't have any storerooms at all. But God feeds them. You are worth much more than birds!" (Luke 12:6–24;NIrV).

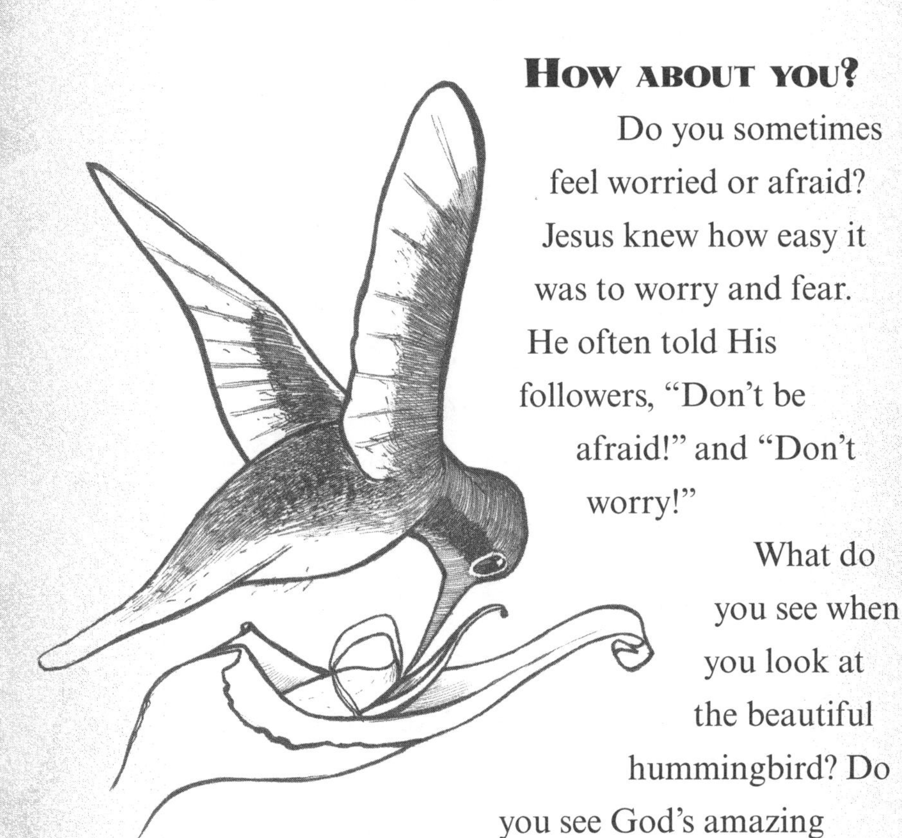

How about you?

Do you sometimes feel worried or afraid? Jesus knew how easy it was to worry and fear. He often told His followers, "Don't be afraid!" and "Don't worry!"

What do you see when you look at the beautiful hummingbird? Do you see God's amazing design in this tiny bird? Does it remind you how important YOU are to God? Look at how God takes care of birds. Watch them fly. Hear them sing. Trust that God takes good care of you. He even knows when one of your hairs falls out!

Memory Verse:

But the very hairs of your head are all numbered. Do not fear.
(Luke 12:7)

Time Changes Things

There are still many horses and ponies today which are no longer under human control, such as the semi-wild ponies of England.

When these young male ponies reach two or three years of age, the head stallion chases them out of the family group. The ponies set out with a few other young males, to roam on their own until they grow up. In a few years, these young stallions will feel strong enough to challenge another head stallion for his mares. Sooner or later, each pony will be head of a large family of mares.

Then one day *he* will chase the young male ponies out of *his* family herd. He will watch them leave on the same journey he made years before.

In the Bible . . .

Many painful changes happened in Joseph's life (Genesis chapters 37–50). His brothers felt jealous of him. They grabbed him and threw him into a pit. When traders came by on their way to Egypt, the brothers sold Joseph. He was taken to Egypt to work as a slave.

It was a hard time for Joseph when his brothers sold him into slavery as a young man. But later, God made Joseph a ruler in Egypt. He was able to bring his family to Egypt and care for them during a famine. In the end, Joseph's painful departure turned into a blessing. It was part of God's good plan to keep His people alive.

How about you?

Can you think of something painful in your life that has turned into a blessing?

We all experience departures from loved ones sometimes. But, for those who love and follow Jesus, God will never fail to turn those partings into blessings, even if it takes a long time.

Experiencing changes is also one way you grow up and become wiser. During times of change you will see God's faithfulness. God is the only One who can make bad things work for good.

Memory Verse:

Joseph told his brothers: "But as for you, you meant evil against me; but God meant it for good . . . to save many people alive."
(Genesis 50:20)

Warning! Watch Out!

The little ladybug that you see flying or crawling in your back yard is sometimes called the "ladybird beetle." With its bright red back and round black spots, the ladybird beetle is a bright and beautiful bug.

But to birds and other predators, those red and black colors on the ladybug's back are warning signals: *Warning! Watch out! You'll be sorry if you eat me! I taste terrible!*

Although ladybirds don't make a good meal for birds, many people appreciate ladybugs. The ladybugs are good at pest control. They eat aphids, which are tiny green bugs that feed on many garden plants like broccoli, cabbage, and tomatoes. Without the ladybug to eat these pests, many vegetable plants might not survive.

There are over 4,000 species of ladybug in the world. Some have two black spots on their back. Others have seven. Some ladybugs have more.

In the Bible . . .

Jesus gave us a warning: "Watch out! Be on guard against wanting to have more and more things. Life is not made up of how much a person has."

Then Jesus told this story:

"A certain rich man's land produced a good crop. He thought to himself, 'What should I do? I don't have any place to store my crops.'

"Then he said, '. . . I will tear down my storerooms and build bigger ones. I will store all my grain and my other things in them. I'll say to myself, "You have plenty of good things stored away for . . . years. Take life easy. Eat, drink and have a good time." '

"But God said to him, 'You foolish man! This very night I will take your life away from you. Then who will get what you have prepared for yourself?'

"That is how it will be for anyone who stores things away for himself but is not rich in God's eyes" (Luke 12:14–21;NIrV).

How about you?

Why do all of us need Jesus' warning about being greedy? Do your possessions, sports, or fun activities keep you away from worshiping God or reading your Bible? Do you think more of *getting* than of *giving*? How can you be a generous giver today?

What is most important to you? Do you think God sees you as *rich* in His eyes?

Memory Verse:

Jesus said, "Watch out! Be on your guard against wanting to have more and more things. Life is not made up of how much a person has."
(Luke 12:15;NIrV)

Help Your Enemy

Crocodiles are a fierce enemy to many animals and birds. They are some of the world's most dangerous predators. A crocodile will lie quietly in muddy water for hours. They look like a scaly log with huge teeth. They wait in ambush for a water bird or an animal that comes down to the river for a drink.

But this fierce crocodile will let a small bird land on its head. In fact, the crocodile opens its mouth and holds its jaws very still. Then the little bird pecks at the food scraps in between the crocodile's teeth!

The crocodile seems to know that it needs the bird's partnership. The bird eats a tasty dinner. And the crocodile gets its teeth cleaned.

This is an example of two very different creatures that live together in a close relationship. Both of them benefit from each other. This is called symbiosis (sym-bi-o-sis). When the bird provides dental care for its natural enemy, it is also being protected by the fierce crocodile.

In the Bible . . .

Jesus wants us to love our enemies. He said, "Here is what I tell you . . . Love your enemies. Do good to those who hate you. Bless those who call down curses on you . . . pray for those who treat you badly. . . . Give to everyone who asks you. And if anyone takes what belongs to you, don't ask to get it back.

"Do to others as you want them to do to you. . . . Lend . . . without expecting to get anything back. Then you . . . will be sons of the Most High God. He is kind to people who are evil and are not thankful. So have mercy, just as your Father has mercy" (Luke 6:27–36;NIrV).

What about you?

Is there someone who has done or said mean things to you? How will you show God's forgiveness and love to them this week? Think about how you can be kind to someone who is mean to other people. Take time to pray for someone who has hurt you or others. Remember that God loves and gives to you, even when you don't deserve it.

Memory Verse:

Jesus said, "Whatever you want men to do to you, do also to them."
(Matthew 7:12)

Living on Little

Leopards are very resourceful cats. They know how to make do with what they have.

For instance, many big cats need large patches of dense brush or thick trees in which to hide from other cats or larger enemies. But the leopard, with its long body and shorter legs, hides with its body close to the ground in wide-open spaces.

As the leopard hides in small shrubs, dips in the ground, or clumps of grass, it easily watches its prey without ever being discovered.

Leopards can actually live where there is very little water at all. In the desert places, leopards live on the water found in the bodies of the prey they eat.

Leopards will often drag their prey up a tree. They tuck it in a fork in the branches. Then it is out of reach of lions, hyenas, and other rivals.

In the Bible . . .

Just as leopards make do with what they have, Jesus used what He had.

Once, when Jesus knew that a crowd was hungry, He used one boy's lunch to feed everyone. How many loaves of bread would you need to feed 5,000 people? 200? 300? How about two fish and 5 loaves of bread? That's all Jesus needed.

"When all of them had enough to eat, Jesus spoke to his disciples, 'Gather the leftover pieces,' he said. 'Don't waste anything.'

"So they gathered what was left over from the

five barley loaves. They filled 12 baskets with the pieces left by those who had eaten" (John 6:12–13;NIrV).

How about you?

Remember that God sent Jesus to be our "Bread of Life." If you have Jesus, you have all that you really need. He gives us life that never ends.

You might feel that you don't have much to give other people. Remember how many people were fed with one boy's lunch? Don't forget that God is able to multiply every little thing *you* give — whether it is your time, your money, your prayers, or your love.

Little is much when God is in it.

Memory Verse:

Jesus said, "I am the living bread which came down from heaven. If anyone eats of this bread, he will live forever."
(John 6:51)

Rejoice Always!

The Red-eyed Vireo is an amazing little bird about six inches long. It is the one bird that sings non-stop throughout the summer!

Singing takes a lot of energy. Most birds rest during the hottest hours of a summer day. But not this cheerful vireo. It sings from dawn to dusk, day after day.

The vireo's song is *not* the most beautiful of all bird songs. But the vireo sings with such persistence! This little bird just won't give up. Nobody can ignore its presence. They are the most common woodland birds in eastern North America. They migrate to South America in the fall. Some of them fly over 3,000 miles. When they return in early spring, guess what: they start singing immediately! And they don't quit until they leave in the fall!

In the Bible . . .

Once three enemy armies came against Judah. King Jehoshaphat called together the people and prayed: "Our God . . . We don't have the power to face this huge army. . . . We don't know what to do. But we're looking to you to help us."

God told the people, "Do not be afraid. Do not lose hope . . . The battle is not yours. It is mine. . . . You will not have to fight . . . Go out and face them tomorrow. I will be with you."

The next day the men who praised God were put in front of the army. They sang as they all marched out to the battlefield, "Give thanks to the Lord. His faithful love continues forever."

And when they began to sing and praise, God brought confusion into the enemy camps. All the enemy soldiers killed each other before Jehoshaphat's people arrived! (2 Chronicles 20:1–30;NIrV).

What about you?

Have you ever had a day when everything went wrong? You probably felt like yelling, slamming a door, or going to bed for a week!

Here's God's solution for a hard day: "Always be joyful . . . Give thanks no matter what happens. God wants you to thank him because you believe in Christ Jesus" (1 Thessalonians 5:16–18;NIrV).

Next time things go wrong, remember Jehoshaphat and the vireo. Instead of getting mad, give thanks to God for His good gifts in your life.

Memory Verse:

In everything give thanks; for this is the will of God in Christ Jesus for you.
(1 Thessalonians 5:18)

Be a Blessing!

The oxpecker is a bird that spends its life serving wild animals in Africa. Oxpeckers help by eating harmful insects and parasites off the bodies of large animals like warthogs, water buffalo, and rhinos.

A warthog can't remove a tick from its own nose. A water buffalo can't keep the fly larvae from crawling into its ears. So these little birds perform a great service by getting rid of many fleas, ticks, and maggots that pester and bite.

The oxpeckers' long claws and stiff tails help them climb up the neck of a giraffe or hang on to a galloping buffalo.

Their heavy flat beaks pull out ticks that have burrowed between the hairs on a warthog. Their strong claws help them hold on as they hunt for flies and fly larvae.

And all the wild animals give these helpful birds freedom to wander all over their bodies. They even let the oxpecker poke its beak up their nose and ears!

In the Bible . . .

Jesus told a story about a man who was a blessing to someone in need.

"A man was going down from Jerusalem. . . . Robbers attacked him. They stripped off his clothes and beat him. Then they went away, leaving him almost dead."

Two religious people walked right by the hurt man and did not help him.

"A Samaritan came to the place. . . . When he saw

the man, he felt sorry for him. He . . . poured olive oil and wine on his wounds and bandaged them. Then he put the man on his own donkey. He took him to an inn and took care of him."

Then Jesus said, "Go and do as [the Samaritan] did."

How about you?

Are you a blessing? What have you done this week to serve someone else? Think about which person in your family needs your help the most. What are some ways you can help them this week? Are you quick to serve? Or do your parents always have to *remind* you to do your chores? Do something kind today without being asked.

Memory Verse:

Through love serve one another . . . You shall love your neighbor as yourself.
(Galatians 5:17)

SMALL, BUT IMPORTANT

Snails may be small and slow, but they play a mighty big role in the recycling of all the dead leaves on our forest floors. Without the work of little creatures like snails, our forests would soon be buried in dead leaves and twigs.

Some kinds of snails eat green plants instead of dead leaves. These snails do great damage to native vegetation in countries like Hawaii. Depending on its species, the snails can be either beneficial or destructive. They can make a good difference or a bad difference where they live.

If you find a snail, place it on a piece of glass. Then watch the waves of its muscles that move its "foot" across the glass.

You will see the snail's mouth on the underside of its large "foot." The snail's file-like tongue is covered with tiny teeth. Snails feed by scraping the surface as they crawl. When they are frightened, the snail will pull its foot back into its shell-home.

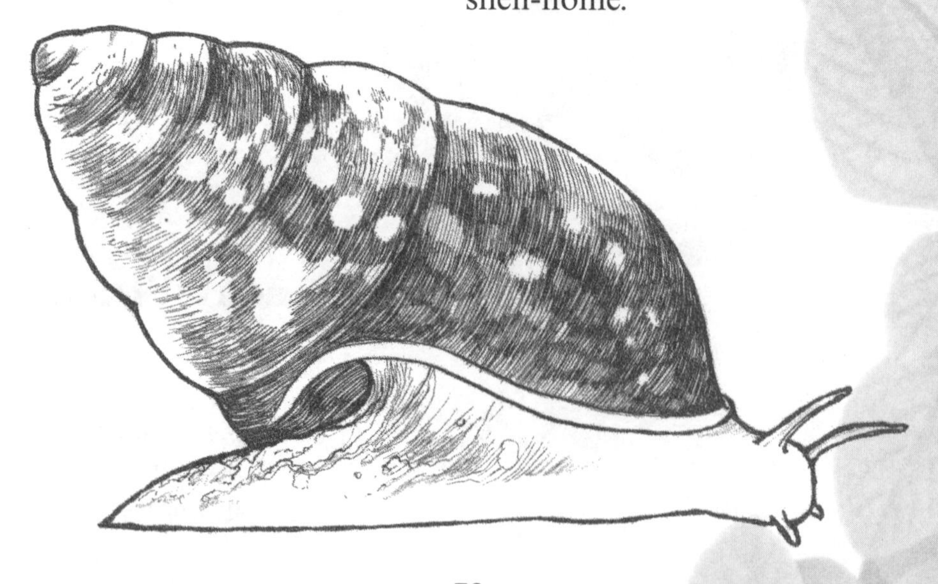

In the Bible . . .

Some people like being big shots. They want to be the first and the most important. They want others to look up to them.

But God sees everything differently than we do. Small things and small people are often used by God for very big purposes . . . like a little snail who has been given the big job of cleaning up the forest floors.

Goliath was a big, strong soldier who came to fight with his sword, spear, and javelin. Another soldier held a shield in front of Goliath. When Goliath saw young David come to fight him with a slingshot, Goliath laughed. Goliath never expected to be defeated by anyone. But God used David, someone much smaller and younger, to beat Goliath (1 Samuel 17:37–54).

What about you?

Do you believe that you have an important job to do in God's world? Do you make a good difference in your home? . . . in your neighborhood?

Have you ever given a small child a glass of water? Did that seem important? Well, God said it was. And Jesus promised, "(You) shall by no means lose (your) reward."

Memory Verse:

Jesus said: "Whoever gives one of these little ones only a cup of cold water . . . he shall by no means lose his reward."
(Matthew 10:42)

What a Dad!

Among most fish, birds, and animals, the *mother* is the one who plays the main role in reproduction. But seahorses have an unusual means of caring for their eggs. The *father* gives the most care to his egg-babies until they hatch.

The female seahorse lays from 50 to 400 eggs in the male's brood pouch. This special pouch is located at the front of the father's body.

The father then fertilizes the eggs in his pouch. His pouch keeps them warm and protects them from all danger.

When the eggs are ready to hatch, the father squeezes his pouch. The little seahorses pop out of their home inside the pouch. They come out in batches of about five at a time.

Seahorses are found in shallow ocean water all over the world. Their tails anchor them to sea plants. That keeps them from being tossed about by the waves.

In the Bible . . .

Jesus wants us to trust that our Heavenly Father is the greatest Dad of all! Jesus said, "Ask, and it will be given to you . . . For everyone who asks receives . . . What man is there among you, who if his son asks for bread, will give him a stone? Or if [the son] asks for a fish, will [the father] give him a serpent? If you then, being evil, know how to give good gifts to your children, how much more will your Father who is in heaven give good things to those who ask Him!" (Matthew 7:7–11).

What about you?

God is a Heavenly Father who never fails those who put their trust in Him. God is a father who always keeps His promises. He never leaves you. He hears every prayer.

Do you feel safe and secure in the love and care of your Heavenly Father? If you ever wonder whether God loves you, just remember: "God so loved ______ *(put your own name here)*, that He gave His only begotten Son, that ______ *(put your name here)* should not perish but have everlasting life" (John 3:16).

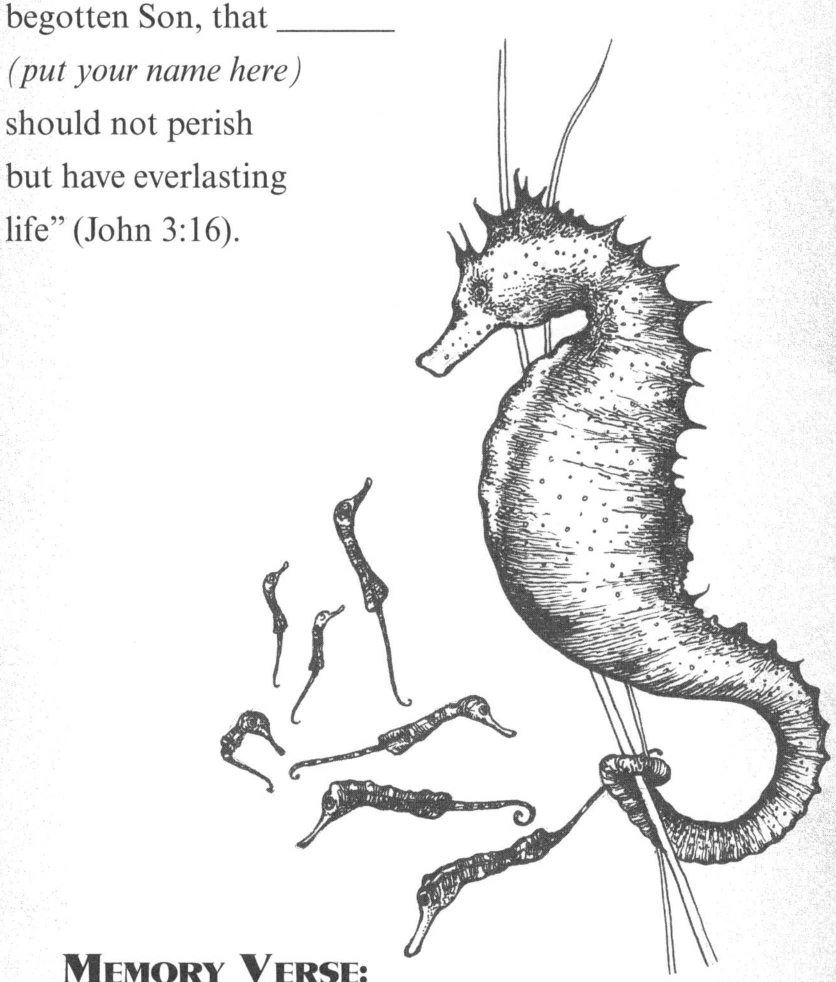

Memory Verse:

In this is love, not that we loved God, but that He loved us and sent His Son.
(1 John 4:10)

Armored Protection

The hard shell of a turtle has two parts — a round covering on top and a flat section under the belly.

Shells come in several shades of browns and greens. Those colors provide camouflage to help protect the turtle from being easily seen.

The shell is made from bony plates that are attached to the turtle's ribs and vertebrae. The strong shell forms a solid covering of armor for the turtle. This protective armor guards the soft body of the turtle from hungry predators. It

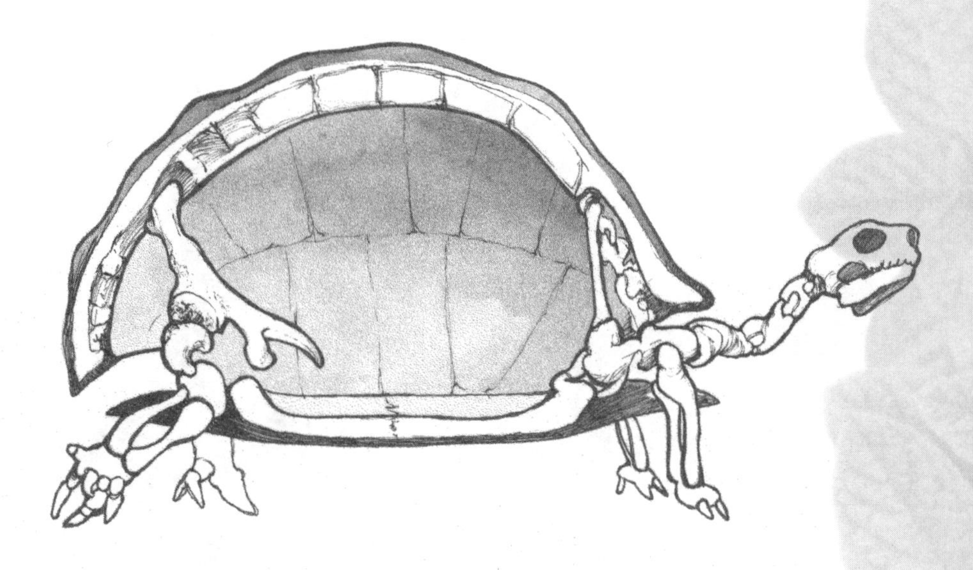

also protects the turtle from bad weather conditions.

A turtle's shell is covered by large scales. They are made out of a tough, horny material. Whenever the turtle is scared, it draws its head and feet back into its shell-home.

In the Bible . . .

The apostle Paul tells us, "Let the Lord make you strong. . . . Put on all of God's armor. Then you can stand firm against the devil's evil plans. Our fight is not against human beings. It is against the rulers, the authorities and the powers of this dark world. . . . So put on all of God's armor. Evil days will come.

"Stand firm. Put the belt of truth around your waist. Put the armor of godliness on your chest. . . . pick up the shield of faith. With it you can put out all of the flaming arrows of the evil one. Put on the helmet of salvation. And take the sword of the Holy Spirit. The sword is God's word" (Ephesians 6:10–17;NIrV).

How about you?

Have you put on God's armor? If so, your shield of faith will protect you so the devil's arrows of doubt and fear won't pierce you. The helmet of salvation will remind you that God has already saved you. Keep reading and memorizing God's Word. It's the *sword* God has given you, and it is your only weapon!

Memory Verse:

Therefore take up the whole armor of God, that you may be able to withstand in the evil day.
(Ephesians 6:13)

Do Your Work Well

Ants, like termites and bees, are social insects. They build a huge nest with many tunnels. Every family of ants has different jobs for the thousands of ants who live within the nest or "colony." All of the ants work together to feed and protect their giant family.

At the center of the nest is the queen's chamber. There is only one queen ant. Her job is to lay eggs — thousands of eggs. The male ants don't live long. They mate with the queen, and then die.

The worker ants divide up the main jobs. Some of them feed and take care of the queen. Other workers take her eggs to the nurseries and keep them warm.

Still other workers take care of eggs when they become larvae. If the nest is disturbed, these workers carry the larvae to safety at another spot.

Still other workers scout out food for everyone. When they do find food, they won't even take a bite for themselves. They carry it back to the nest for everyone to share.

Soldier ants guard the workers who get food. They have large jaws to fight against attackers and defend the nest.

In the Bible . . .

Some people call themselves Christians, but they don't worship with others. And they won't help a fellow Christian. Read what James told these people:

"My brothers and sisters, what good is it if

people claim they have faith but don't act like it? . . . Suppose a brother or sister has no clothes or food. Suppose one of you says to them, 'Go. I hope everything turns out fine for you. Keep warm. Eat well.' And you do nothing about what they really need. Then what good have you done? It is the same with faith. If it doesn't cause us to do something, it's dead.

"The body without the spirit is dead. In the same way, faith without good works is dead" (James 2:14–26;NIrV).

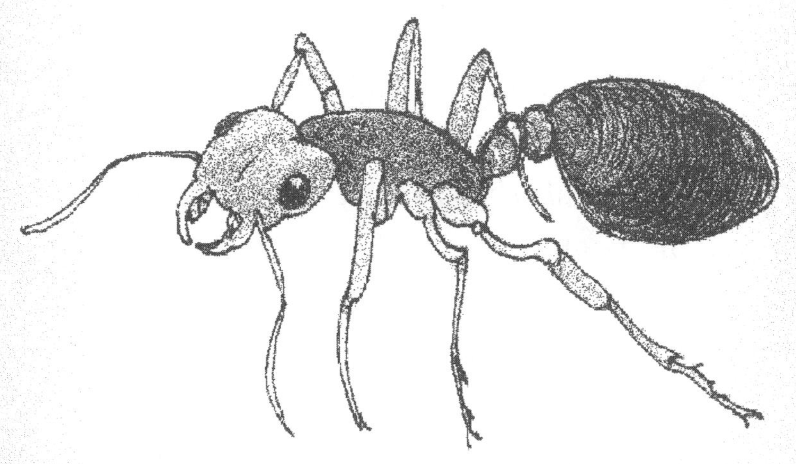

How about you?

Think of three things you can do well. Are you willing to help your family, classmates, and neighbors with the work that needs to be done each day?

Do you care more about yourself . . . or about others? Ask God to show you what your special job is in the body of Christ. Remember the hard-working ants. What *good works* will you do as part of God's team this week?

Memory Verse:

Faith without good works is dead.
(James 2:26)

Love One Another

Small parrots that are often kept in cages as pets are called "budgies," or parakeets. These little birds have a variety of green or blue-colored feathers.

Parakeets like each other's company and are often called "lovebirds." They sit close together on a perch and rub beaks while they chirp at each other. If you hang a small mirror in a cage with a parakeet, it will spend hours cuddled up by the mirror, talking to its own reflection.

As with parrots, the smaller parakeets can learn to "say" words and phrases that they hear the most often.

Parakeets also like to live close to each other in the wild. The monk parakeet from South America builds a nest with a rounded dome at the top. This is usually made out of thorny twigs with an opening at the bottom. Many pairs of birds will build their nests right next to each other. A large group or colony of 20 nests can fill the top of a big tree. The colony then becomes the center of all activities for these social birds.

In the Bible . . .

Before Jesus was crucified, He told His disciples, "Love each other, just as I have loved you. No one has greater love than the one who gives his life for his friends" (John 15:12;NIrV).

The apostle John says, "We know what love is because Jesus Christ gave his life for us. So we should give our lives for our brothers and sisters. Suppose someone sees a brother or sister in need and is able to help them. If he doesn't take pity on them, how can the love of God be in him? Dear children, don't just talk about love. Put your love into action. . . . God has commanded us to believe in . . . his Son Jesus Christ. He has also commanded us to love one another" (1 John 3:16–23;NIrV).

What about you?

How do you show that you love others? Remember that love is not just a "feeling." It is a decision to care for someone. You must make a choice to do what is best for them. Do you know someone who feels lonely? Do you know someone who has troubles? How will you put your love into action today?

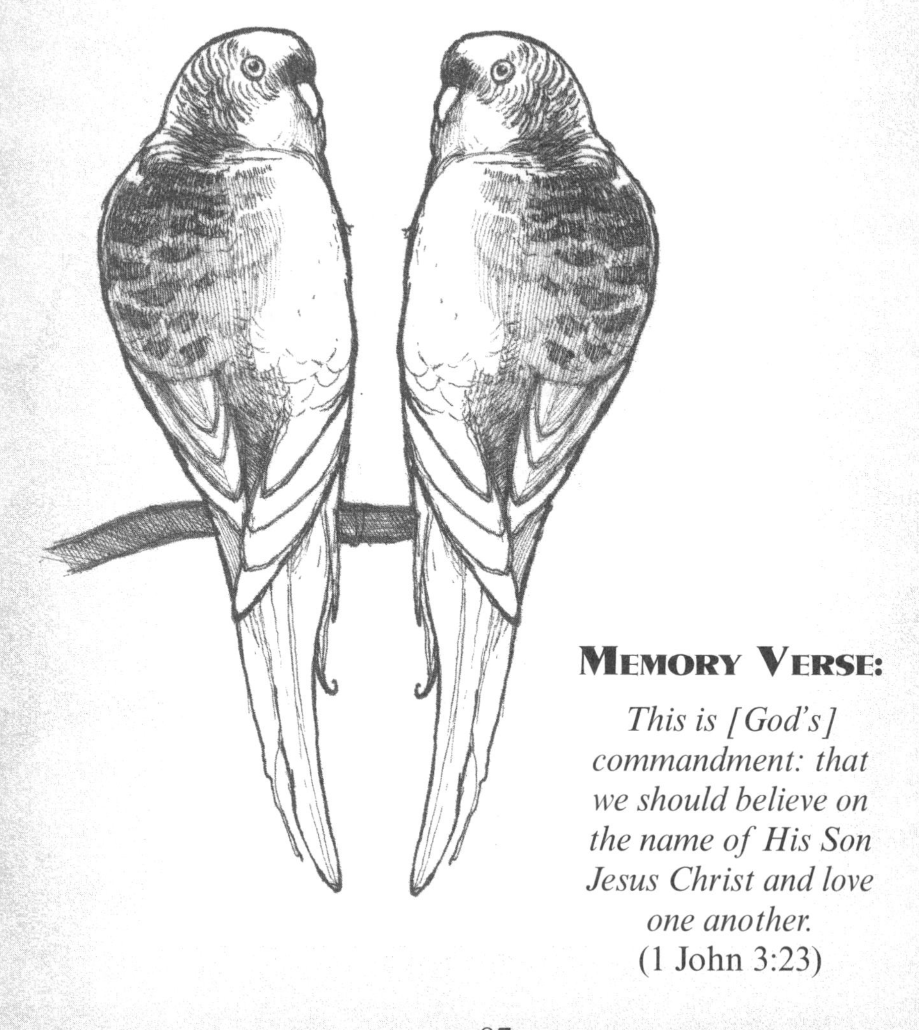

Memory Verse:

This is [God's] commandment: that we should believe on the name of His Son Jesus Christ and love one another.
(1 John 3:23)

I See You!

Crabs have excellent eyesight. Their compound eyes stick up high on stalks at the top of their head. These stalks can also be folded down.

With these good eyes, crabs can see all around at once. They notice everything! They run off quickly when they see enemy birds fly towards them. They also use their good eyesight to spot a mate.

Crabs belong to a group of animals that are protected by a hard skeleton outside of their body. They move on ten legs that have several joints. Most crabs live in the ocean, but they also use their legs to crawl about on shore.

Crabs use their two largest claws to pick up pieces of food. One kind of crab climbs mangrove trees. It turns over the leaves, and, with a quick snap of their pincher, captures flies that are resting in the shade of the leaf.

In the Bible . . .

"The eyes of the Lord run to and fro throughout the whole earth, to show Himself strong on behalf of those whose heart is loyal to Him" (2 Chronicles 16:9).

"The eyes of the Lord are on the righteous, and His ears are open to their cry. The face of the Lord is against those who do evil" (Psalm 34:15–16).

God looks all over to find someone who trusts Him. God wants to show His love and power in the life of that person. He will hear their prayers and help them.

What about you?

Have you hidden something you've done from your parents? Nothing is hidden from God. God's eyes look over the whole earth. When you have done wrong, confess it to God right away. He already knows what you've done. Jesus died to forgive you — just ask for His forgiveness.

God also sees what others have done to hurt you. He knows when you cry. And God knows when you trust Him and do what is right. He sees when you try to get along with someone who is mean to you. And someday, in Heaven, God will wipe every tear from your eyes.

Memory Verse:

Behold the eye of the Lord is on those who fear Him, on those who hope in His mercy.
(Psalm 33:18)

GENEROUS "DOCTORS"

In order to stay healthy, fish in the ocean need to be cleaned regularly. Somehow larger fish like the grouper fish know that they need regular "checkups." So they line up for "surgery" done by little "doctors" called *cleaner fish*.

Tiny "cleaners" nibble away pests, parasites, and dead skin on the bodies of groupers and other fish. The cleaners also work inside the gills and the mouth of larger fish. They can even work safely down the throat of a shark!

You might wonder why larger fish don't gobble up the cleaners. Scientists have watched the little fish flip sideways, flutter their fins, and perform unusual dances. These special movements seem to stop larger fish from eating them.

As payment for their good work, cleaners receive free meals. (They actually *like* to eat dead skin and parasites!) So they receive benefits also when they help and give.

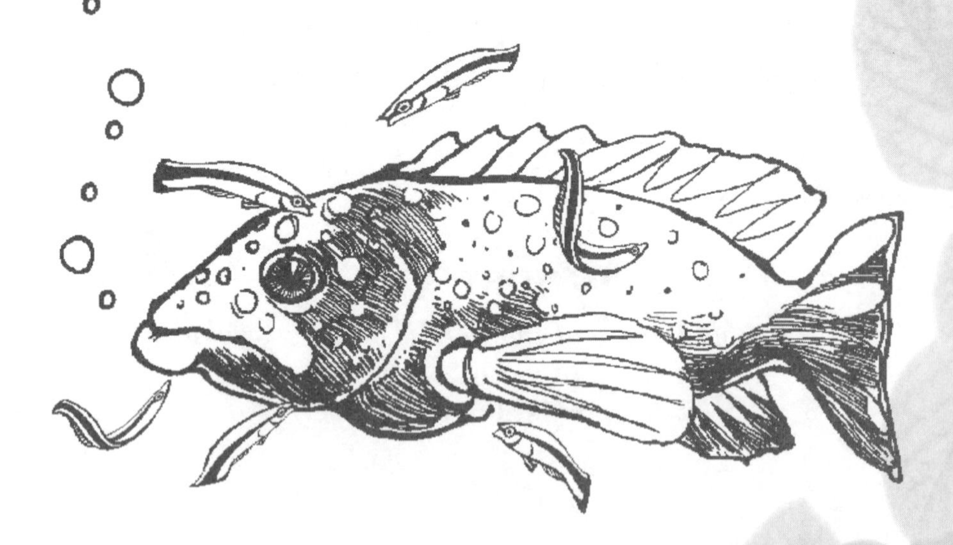

In the Bible . . .

Just like small cleaner fish help and do good to larger "enemy" fish, so Jesus wants us to live as generous givers.

Jesus said, "Love your enemies. Do good to them. Lend to them without expecting to get anything back. Then you will receive a lot in return. . . . Give, and it will be given to you. A good amount will be poured into your lap. It will be pressed down, shaken together, and running over. The same amount you give will be measured out to you" (Luke 6:35–38;NIrV)

How about you?

In what ways have you been generous to a person who has been mean to you? Think of three ways you can *give* to people in your family . . . and others in your neighborhood.

When you give of your time and effort, you can be sure God will give back to you the same way you give to others. And remember: "God loves a cheerful giver" (2 Corinthians 9:7).

Memory Verse:

Jesus said, "Give to everyone who asks of you. . . . Give, and it will be given to you."
(Luke 6:30–38)

No Vacancy!

Most crabs are totally protected by a hard outer exoskeleton, but the hermit crab has a softer body. The back part of its jointed shell is *not* protected or armored. Because of this lack of protection on its abdomen, the hermit crab needs to find a hard shell in which to hide.

The hermit crab looks for discarded seashells. Old mollusk shells are perfect "homes." The hermit crab backs almost completely into the empty shell. Using the small hook at the end of its tail, the crab secures itself inside the shell. The crab's large claws and pincer guard the opening.

As the crab grows, its body casing splits and falls off, making a new, larger casing. This forces the crab to search for a larger home.

Spiral triton shells are a favorite shelter of hermit crabs, but it is hard to find big, empty shells. Large hermit crabs end up fighting over them. They duel

with their pincers . . . and the winner moves into the new home.

In the Bible . . .

Like the hermit crab continually changes homes, so your life will always be changing. Change is part of growing. Only one thing never changes — God. "I am the Lord. I do not change" (Malachi 3:6;NIrV).

Jesus gave us this promise: "There are many rooms in my Father's house. If this were not true, I would have told you. I am going there to prepare a place for you. If I go and do that, I will come back. And I will take you to be with me" (John 14:2–3;NIrV).

How about You?

How many different houses have you lived in? Don't forget that someday you will have a new home in heaven. Life on earth doesn't last long. Even if you lived to be 100 years old, what is that compared to eternal life that never ends?

Read Revelation, chapters 21 and 22. Think about the home Jesus prepared for you in heaven. Once you're there, you'll never move again!

Memory Verse:

Here we do not have a city that lasts. But we are looking for the city that is going to come.

(Hebrews 13:14;NirV)

Deep Roots

If you have read through this entire book, then something has happened to you. You have planted God's Word in your mind and heart. Your *roots of faith* have grown.

It is like planting a bean seed in the garden. You can't see the roots, but they are the first things to grow. The small white "fingers" poke out of the seed in search of food.

The fat seed also feeds a tiny shoot that grows up toward the sunlight. When the shoot breaks through the soil, it grows two leaves that turn green in the sunlight.

As the roots reach down in the dirt, they take in food and water from the soil. Now the bean seed shrivels and shrinks. Its food supply has been used up. It is no longer needed. The tangle of deep roots will find food for the growing stem and leaves.

With deeper roots, the plant has a better chance to live during hot summer days.

In the Bible . . .

God wants your faith to grow, just like a seed always grows when you plant it. Strong faith helps God's people make it through tough times. Think of people in the Bible whose "roots" of faith were deep: Moses, Elijah, David, Joshua, Peter, the apostle Paul. They needed deep roots of faith to face their problems.

"You received Christ Jesus as Lord. So keep on living in him. Have your roots in him. Build yourselves up in him. Grow strong in what you believe, just as you were taught" (Colossians 2:6–8;NIrV).

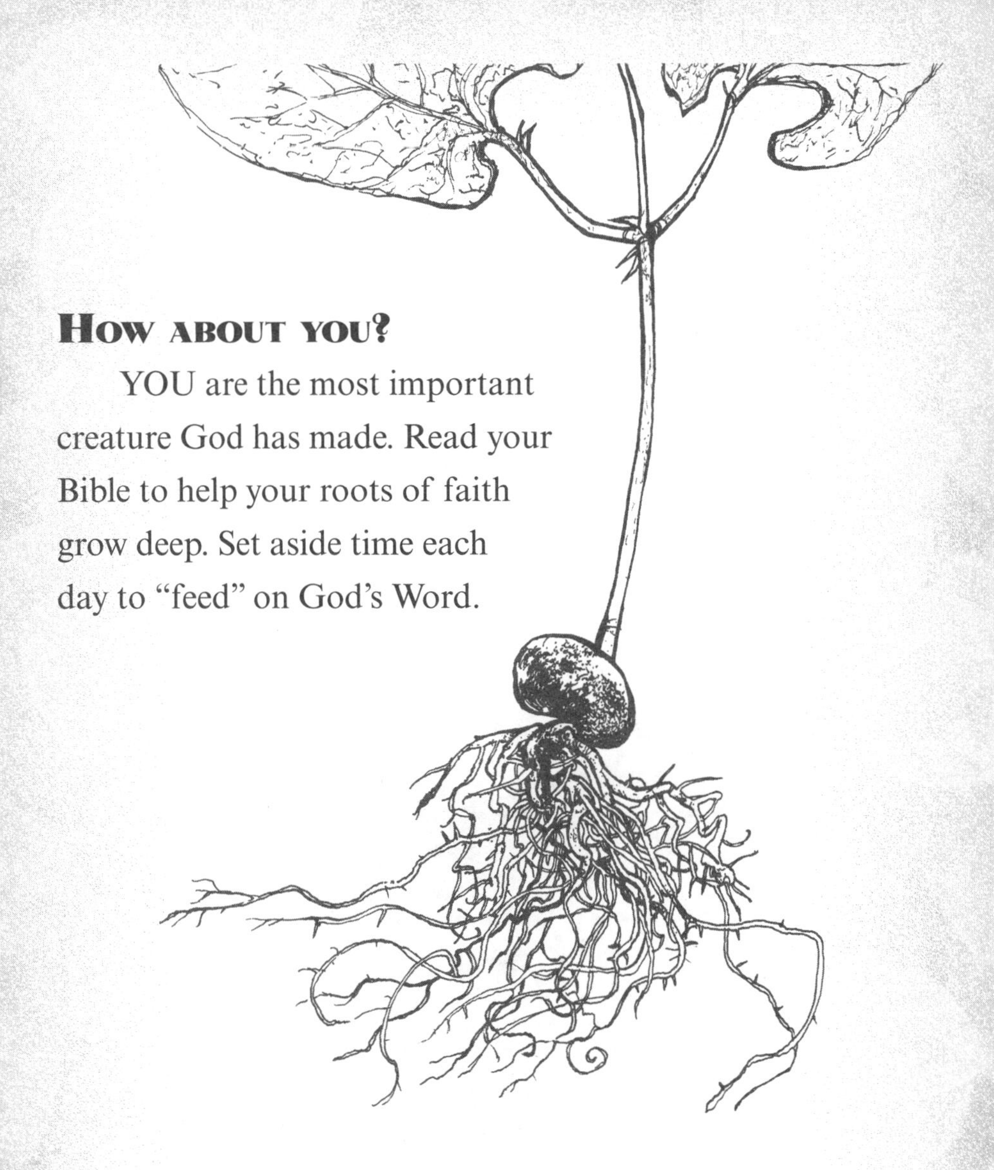

How about you?

YOU are the most important creature God has made. Read your Bible to help your roots of faith grow deep. Set aside time each day to "feed" on God's Word.

Be like the bean plant. Deepen your roots of faith. Reach out to God in prayer every day. You need a strong faith so you won't give up when you face problems and times of trouble.

Memory Verse:

As you . . . have received Christ Jesus the Lord,
so walk in Him, rooted and built up in Him
and established in the faith.
(Colossians 2:6–7)

The End

Don't Stop Here!

read on...

Creation | Grades 1-4

God Made the World and Me
Preschool

The Creation Story for Children | All Ages

Great resources to help build your child's Biblical worldview by

The Haidles and Master Books®